The Way Of The
HUMMINGBIRD

In Legend, History &
Today's Gardens

Virginia C. Holmgren

Capra Press
SANTA BARBARA
1986

Cover design by Barbara Sowle
Designed and typeset in Baskerville by Jim Cook
SANTA BARBARA, CALIFORNIA

LIBRARY OF CONGRESS CATALOGING IN PUBLICATION DATA
Holmgren, Virginia C.
THE WAY OF THE HUMMINGBIRD
Bibliography: p.   Includes index.
1. Hummingsbirds.   I. Title
QL696.A558H65   1986   598.8'99   86-9721
ISBN 0-88496-250-4

Published by
CAPRA PRESS
Post Office Box 2068
Santa Barbara, California 93120

Table of Contents

Acknowledgements

Sincere thanks are hereby offered the many librarians who helped in my research for this book, especially those of the Multnomah County Library of Portland, Oregon, including Clyde Marshall, Betty Johnson, Fern Kenyon, Barbara Kahl and others who are appreciated though unnamed; E.E. Larson of the Hispanic Division, Library of Congress; Marilyn Kierstead of Reed College Library; Linda L. Reichert of the American Museum of Natural History; various staff members of the libraries of the University of Virginia; Linda Hall Library in Kansas City, Missouri; University of Oregon; University of Portland; Oregon Historical Society; University of California; San Francisco State University; Heard Museum of Phoenix, Arizona; Peabody Museum of Harvard University; Jamestown-Yorktown Foundation, Jamestown, Virginia; Portland Audubon Society.

Also thanks for sharing personal books or knowledge are due Bernice Baldwin, William Bullard, Bert Raynes, Zean Moore, Jean C. Taylor, Professor Richard Schultz of the Foreign Language Department, Portland State University, Bruce Hamilton of the Oregon Historical Society, Professor William A. Calder III, Biology Department, University of Arizona, and Mace Perona.

FRONT COVER:
Ruby-throated Hummingbird, by Alexander Wilson, Philadelphia, ca. 1871. Male at right.

1.

HUMMINGBIRD CHALLENGE THEN AND NOW

A HUMMINGBIRD COMES darting into your garden, feathers gleaming like jewels in the sunlight. With wings a-whir it hovers over a flower, thrusts out long beak and tongue to probe for nectar, takes its fill and backs off, turning with a half-somersault whirl to go on to another flower, and another. You watch in wonder, not knowing whether to marvel most at elfin size, jewel colors, acrobatic skill or a hum-tune that comes from fast-beating wings instead of a throat. But you do know that this hummer is different from all other birds. The more you watch, the more you feel challenged to understand its ways. And along with all the other marvels that demand explanation is the way a ruby-red gorget can turn to drab, all in an instant, as if touched by magic.

Magic! In today's world such answers must come from science, not magic. But long ago—when ancient Amerind people were the only humans in the land where our gardens now grow—magic was the only way to meet the hummingbird challenge with satisfying response.

Many a tale of hummingbird magic can be found among the ancient legends of American Indian tribes. But not one such story would ever have been told if the people of those times had let hummers wing by without feeling a stir of wonder, a compelling urge to understand the reasons behind their unusual ways.

That same wonder, that same insistent questioning of how and why, is still present in the many scientific studies of hummingbird actions and appearance published in modern reference books and ornithological journals. Today's scientists seeking explanations through factual research believe everything in nature—however mysterious and magical it may seem—is the reasonable result of some logical natural cause. The cause may be difficult to find, but they are convinced it is there. The ancient Indians puzzling over these same mysteries believed they were caused by supernatural spirit-beings who possessed that inexplicable force called 'magic.' Thus empowered, the spirits could change man or bird or beast as they pleased with reward or punishment or merely as a playful whim. So, although both the Indians of old and today's scientists have felt the same challenge to explain hummingbirds, each has looked for answers from a different viewpoint.

In spite of this difference, the reasoning behind two sets of answers is often closely akin. Indian storytellers of long ago—Creek, Cherokee, Menomini, Navaho, Yurok and many others—wove tales of magic about hummingbirds' swift flight and fast wing-beat without the proof of precise measurements that Crawford Greenwalt and other experts can now provide with today's electronic equipment. Yet both the legend weavers and Greenwalt agree that hummer wing movements are too fast for the human eye to measure.

More than a few legends contain a reminder of the ancient belief that birds and beasts and people once understood each other perfectly, talked together and shared their problems. Modern science doesn't go quite that far, but it does offer ample proof that most wild creatures do understand the danger signals of other species and obey their warning. So when deer browsing in a thicket slip away quietly if they hear the chittering alarm cries of a hummingbird, there is material both for weaving a Navaho legend and for making a factual report on inter-species communication.

Any tale of humans who talk to animals—and get answers—is now considered sheer fabrication by most people. But there is increasing proof that many animal sounds and actions are meaningful communication, not just mere noise and idle movement, and that people can translate at least some of these messages if they try. Communication between hummingbirds and humans had one verified instance in Jamaica a few years ago when tourists were invited to watch hummingbirds in a certain garden every afternoon at four o'clock. The old woman who owned the garden would have syrup feeders ready and anyone with a hopeful dollar to spend could sit with feeder in hand and wait for hummers to appear. And suddenly, there they were — especially the Streamertails, alias Long-tailed Doctor Birds, Jamaica's official national bird.

"How do they know to come at four o'clock?" the amazed tourists would ask.

And with a grin and a shrug the old woman gave her answer: "I tell them!"

And of course she did—not with words, but with actions, her daily offering of sweet syrup just at the time all sensible hummingbirds begin to think of storing up enough nectar to see them through the night.

Actions—and perhaps an undefinable something more— explain the communication between another elderly hummer-watcher in Carmel Highlands, California—botanist Lester Rowntree—and a hummingbird that had been hatched in her garden, affectionately dubbed "Baby" and made welcome with food, protection and daily visits. One day in 1976 when a full-grown Baby was building her own nest, a friend happened to be on hand to witness their exchange. Using a sweet, shrill voice, the woman called invitingly: "Baby! Baby! Want another gray hair for your nest?" No sooner had she plucked the offered hair than the hummer was there to snatch it up and whirl away to the hedge where the new doll-cup nest was ready for soft lining.

"She understood you!" the visitor said in bemused wonder, certain the story would bring more doubting listeners than believers.

Anyone who has ever seen a hummer nest is quite ready to believe these birds are expert builders. The cup shape, small size and outer covering of moss and plant fibers are perfect camouflage, making the nest seem just another cluster of windblown foliage caught on a jutting twig. Ornithologist William Calder, working in the Colorado Rockies where even summer nights are cold, testifies that many nests are placed so overhanging leaves or branches deflect any chilling night wind. Also, thermal testing has proved that the carefully woven layers provide remarkable insulation for eggs or young and the mother who must guard them whatever the weather. Ancient Indians had no thermometers to make such tests, but they knew and admired the hummingbirds' superior architectural skills. In one Maya legend, birds who asked a tribal Wise Man how to build a sturdy nest were sent to the hummingbirds for lessons.

As the legends show, ancient storytellers sometimes depended on their own powers of observation instead of magic to explain hummingbird wonders. And many a modern scientist who cannot find a logical explanation for every quandary may wish he could let magic bring the same easy solution as in days of old.

2.

How The Legends Began

In ancient times, nature's puzzles were first explored by test and touch and keen watching. When even the most careful observation did not reveal a clear "this-causes-that" reason, observers assumed that magic was involved. Some god or spirit-being had obviously chosen to use the mysterious power no human could muster. Such wonder-tales of magic have been told in every land the world around. But, tales of hummingbird magic were told only in the Americas, since wild hummingbirds have never lived free anywhere else. Even in captivity, few have lived for long elsewhere.

For all time, these tiny birds with long needle-like bills and brilliant changeable colors have made their home only in North and South America, on the isthmus that now links these two continents and on the islands roundabout their shores. Here in this New World hemisphere—and nowhere else—hummingbirds have woven their elf-cup nests of plant down and spider webs, laid their two pearl-like eggs and tended the minikin naked hatchlings that would somehow grow into feathered wonders. Observers have marveled at their glittering jewel-bright sheen and the incredible skills that enable them to hover on furiously beating wings, fly forward, backward, or even upside down. Here and nowhere else could watchers listen to the music of those whirring, purring wings and stare in wonder as the radiant colors changed—all in one mysterious moment—to ashen gray or midnight blackness.

In the beginning, American Indians were the only people to see hummingbirds and to ask questions about their mysterious ways. Usually, in each tribe, someone—Wise Woman, Medicine Man or Respected Elder—would hear these questions and answer with an explanation from tribal lore or with a new story if an old one didn't fit. Old or new, the answer usually developed into a story satisfying to all listeners, children and adults alike.

Those ancient Amerind storytellers put their answer-tales together from this and that—as storytellers everywhere have always done. To make up a tale explaining some hummingbird mystery, they began with whatever bit of truth they had gained from their own wondering and watching. Then they knotted this truth into a firm foundation for their story, much the way a basketmaker knots and loops a twist of fiber around the spread-out reeds to make a sturdy base for further weaving. Once that knot of truth was in place, the storytellers worked in whatever strands of tribal lore happened to fit and added anything else that helped round out the tale.

Almost always they found a way to weave in some incident or animal character to serve as a worthwhile lesson or example. Usually they would build some whisper of suspense, too, just to keep everyone listening. Often a detail would make listeners laugh—or at least smile—while another would cause them to nod in agreement. And whenever no reasonable answer could be figured out from the facts at hand, the storyteller would summon up some spirit-being to solve the mystery with a magic touch.

Indians in almost every corner of the Americas told such tales, because hummingbirds can be seen nearly everywhere in the hemisphere either as year-round residents, seasonal visitors or nesters, or occasional wanderers. Since hummers feed only on flower nectar, flower pollen, flowing tree sap and insects, they are most abundant in tropic and semi-tropic lands where flowers and insects can flourish all year. Only a few hardy species are residents in temperate zones year-round, but several more go farther north—or farther south—each summer to nest or wander in temperate zones. The final count of hummingbird species has probably not yet been made. New species are still being discovered in remote Andean valleys and other isolated areas. One was even discovered near Oaxaca, Mexico in 1964, and six tropic species were found in the 1970s. The American Museum of Natural History, in a list edited by J.J. Morony and others in 1975, set the species total at 338. In 1983, Paul Johnsgard in his book, *Hummingbirds of North America,* published by Smithsonian Press, raised the count to 342, but warned some of the newly added species might prove to be hybrids.

Whatever the current tally, more than half the hummingbird species live in South America along the equator. According to Johnsgard, Ecuador has the most with 163 species; but Colombia with 135 and Peru with 100, Venezuela with 97 and Brazil with 90 are close behind. Other authors give slightly different figures, but all agree that each area has species seen nowhere else. The number decreases in lands farther south into the temperate zone. Chile has seven, Uruguay just four and Tierra del Fuego has only one, the Green-backed Firecrown.

Northward from the equator, over 50 species can be seen almost anywhere from Panama to Mexico. But that score is instantly cut in half when you cross the Rio Grande into the United States. Even including rare wanderers and a few species seen only in scattered areas close to the Mexican border, the total hummingbird species recorded north of the U.S.-Mexico border is just 24. North of the Canadian-U.S. boundary the number slips to five. (See Chapter 7 for list.)

Only one species—the Ruby-throated Hummingbird—nests in states east of the Mississippi, although it ranges farther west in Canada. Also, only one species—the Rufous Hummingbird—nests in Alaska and the Yukon territory, although other species occasionally visit the Far North on summer wanderings. Only one species—the Anna's Hummingbird—is exclusively a north-of-Mexico resident, a non-migrating northerner that only occasionally nests or visits in Mexico.

All known hummer species are really small in comparison with other birds, except for one from western South America. Even this large one—although it is named Giant Hummingbird—is barely over eight inches in length, about the size of a Barn Swallow. A few other species measure five or six inches,

Grant Hummingbird, from Ridgway, 1890.

but most are under four inches from beak tip to tail end—not even as long as a Bald Eagle's middle toe! Several are under three inches. The smallest of all—the smallest bird in the world—is the 2½-inch Bee Hummingbird found only on Cuba and the nearby Isle of Pines. However, this species wasn't discovered and classified until 1850. Until that date,

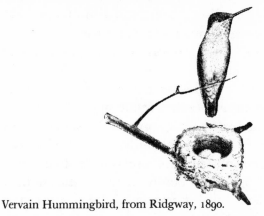

Vervain Hummingbird, from Ridgway, 1890.

the Vervain Hummingbird known since 1758 on Jamaica, Haiti and Puerto Rico, was counted the smallest at 2½ to 2¾ inches. The smallest species regularly nesting north of Mexico is the Calliope Hummingbird identified in 1847. The Bumblebee Hummingbird on record in 1839 is found from Mexico to Panama and is suspected of crossing over into California now and then. Like the Vervain, these two are the same 2½ to 2¾ inches in length.

Compare any of these smallest hummingbirds with the ostrich, the world's largest living bird, and you discover that each hummer—beak tip to tail end—is just about the size of an ostrich's eye! Compare ostrich and hummingbird eggs, and you also have the world's largest and smallest. But the ostrich hen is sixty times the weight of her egg, while the little female hummer is only eight times her egg weight. From her viewpoint, it is a very large egg and producing two for each setting must require formidable strength and endurance.

Many hummer species, north and south, have much the same coloring as the familiar male Ruby-throated, with bright red gorget (throat), emerald-green back and white front. Other males,and some females, may have throat ruffs of bright blue, green, purple or orange instead of ruby red, and coats of copper, bronze or bluish tones rather than emerald green. The male and female of some species have different coloring and so are often mistaken for two different species. Beaks of some hummers are straight. Others curve, either slightly or deeply, and all vary in length. Tails, too, may be short, medium or long, plain or with fancy trim.

In spite of all this variety in form and coloring, most of the old Indian legends told of "the" hummingbird—as if there were only one kind. This is a handy storyteller's device to avoid the clutter of unnecessary details and to get right to the question that had called for a story in the first place. After all, most of the questions were about hummingbirds' small size, brilliant colors, unusual flying skills and feeding habits. And since all members of the family are much alike in these matters, a tale about "the" hummingbird was satisfactory enough. Besides, in some areas only one kind of hummingbird existed, or at least only one kind that was common.

Some of these ancient tales were told only a few times— perhaps even just once—and then forgotten. No tribe had a written language to keep any tale on a word-for-word permanent record. If a storyteller died before anyone else memorized his tale, it could never be told again exactly the same way. Many tribes kept a record of sorts, with paintings on tanned skins or pottery, or carved figures of wood or stone, or scratched-out rock figures as reminders of tribal history or legends. But for the most part, legends were left to the good memories of tribal elders who had an uncanny skill in passing down such lore from one generation to the next, year after year, even century after century. Nevertheless, some things were forgotten or changed on purpose when a new storyteller thought an improvement was in order. The more often a story was told, the more likely some change would be made. And even the best-remembered tales were usually known to only one tribe—and would be forgotten forever if the tribe were exterminated by warfare or illness.

In time, the white-skinned foreigners came across the sea to usurp Indian lands and destroy much of tribal customs and traditions. But they did keep written records of what they saw and heard of Indian ways, and thus they preserved many of the ancient legends that otherwise might have been lost.

With these legends at hand we can look for knowledge of hummingbird ways in this Indian lore as well as in modern research. And it is no great surprise to discover that the wondering questions asked and answered in the legends are not entirely different from those studied in the latest scientific research.

3.

HUMMINGBIRDS IN
LEGEND AND SCIENCE

THROUGH ALL WRITTEN records of hummingbird history—
from Columbus to the present century—runs much the same
thread of marvel at the mysterious ways of the hummingbirds. Over and over, for nearly five hundred years, the same
questions have been asked: Why are hummingbirds so small,
so radiantly beautiful, and why is their behavior so amaz-
ingly different from that of other birds?

For thousands of years longer, American Indians have
asked the same questions and heard their Wise Ones give
answers fashioned from what is now called folklore and
legend. Seven questions have been asked most often, and in
this chapter these seven are now asked again—and each one
answered first with tales from ancient legends and then from

today's scientific studies. Readers can learn from both interpretations because Indian storytellers and today's scientists have all been perplexed by the same puzzles and have found their answers in close observations of hummingbirds.

These legends have all been told many times before. They are re-tellings based on still older re-tellings recorded by the U.S. Bureau of Ethnology from 1879 to 1916, for the most part, or on other twentieth century records of tribal members or scholars. When more than one version of an old tale has been found, something from each has been woven into this new telling, along with whatever added background seems important for today's readers. No legend here is a word-for-word duplication of any published text, yet each one is told with concern for keeping the aura of the original narration.

1. Why are hummingbirds so small, so beautiful and so different from other birds?

From a tale told by the Maya Indians of southern Mexico, Yucatan, Guatemala, Belize, Honduras:

Long and long ago when the world was not quite finished, the Maya Great God looked around the sacred place where he had been making the different kinds of birds. He had made birds of every sort and size, each one good in its own way, and now he thought the making of birds was finished.

But just then he spied a few scraps of grayish feathers, a long thin beak, some tiny bits of bone and muscles and such that had not been used. He could not bear to waste even these small scraps, and so he took them in his hands gently, joining this to that to form the birdshape, and adding the long beak last of all. Then he gave this new small bird the gift of life.

It fluttered its tiny wings, opened its bright black eyes and looked up at its maker. And the Great God smiled down, thinking how small it was, how very small. Smaller than any other bird he had ever made. Even with that long beak it measured no more than the length of a man's thumb!

The Great God frowned, wondering if a shorter beak would have been better, but then shook his head. This small one was designed to feed on the nectar of flowers—good food that no other birds could reach easily—and a long beak was needed. And so was a long tongue that could reach out even beyond the beak tip to flick off bits of yellow pollen dust for added nourishment and to aid in catching insects buried in a flower cup or flitting past in mid-air.

To gather such food, the small one needed unusual flying skills, as well as the long bill and tongue. So the Great God made sure it could fly forward or backward, straight up or straight down, on a zigzag, or even upside down for a quick turnabout, and he also gave it the ability to hover almost endlessly in mid-air. Oh, yes! What this small one lacked in size, it more than made up for in talents.

With an upward toss of his hand, the god sent it flying off to find its place in the world. For a moment it hovered there, just above his fingertips, the wings whirring so fast that the air passing through the feathers played a little humming tune that sounded like *'dzu-nu-ume, dzu-nu-ume!'* The Great God smiled to hear it, for he knew the Mayas would call this smallest one *Dzunuume*, 'The Hummer.'

Of course the Great God knew one bird of a kind is not enough. Every creature has to have its mate. He called on his magic powers and before him were more grayish feathers and tiny bones and a long beak, just like the ones he had used before. He put them all together in the same way and gave this new little bird the gift of life, too, so that *Dzunuume* would have his mate. Then he told the two of them to make this their wedding day and live happily ever after. And off he went to attend to other matters.

Some birds who had been lingering nearby heard the word "wedding" and came fluttering down eager to see the bride and groom and have a part in the celebration. First a sweet-voiced Solitare Thrush offered to sing its flute-like song for their wedding music. Then a gentle breeze came along and began to shake down fragrant flower petals for a carpet. Bright-winged butterflies gathered in a dancing circle to mark out the room. Even some spiders wanted to help and began spinning their most delicate webs to decorate the bridal pathway, telling the bride that she could use them afterward to build her nest. And the great sun overhead held himself ready to send down his rays for a blessing.

"Oh, everything will be so beautiful!" chirped a little brown-streaked House Finch with cap and throat as red as chili peppers. "Everything beautiful for a beautiful bride and a handsome groom. The most beau—"

And then he stopped short, as if he wished he could swallow his tongue or take back the words. For *Dzunuume* and his little mate were not beautiful. Not in the least. Their feathers were a dull, drab gray. No pretty colors at all.

The House Finch looked around at the other birds and the other birds looked back at him, all very much concerned. Something had to be done. Somehow these two small gray ones had to be made beautiful.

The long-tailed Quetzal bird, the most splendid bird in all Maya land, was the first to speak. "Please help yourselves to some of my feathers," he offered, spreading his long green tail plumes.

"And take some of mine, please," called a Violet-green Swallow, skimming low enough for them to pluck the pearl-white feathers from her breast.

The kind offers were accepted the moment they were made. In a trice the bride and groom were feathered in glistening green and white.

"Now you need some of my red feathers for a scarf," exclaimed the House Finch. He promptly gave so many red feathers to *Dzunuume* that he could spare only one or two for the little bride.

Before anyone else could add any other colors, the sun came out from behind a cloud where he had been waiting impatiently and pronounced the two little green-coats married forever and always. For a blessing he sent down his most dazzling rays straight to little *Dzunuume's* throat, making the red scarf feathers flash red and gold like a leaping flame.

"Oh-h-h! Ah-h-h!" cried the birds and butterflies and spiders and the breeze together in wonder.

And then another dazzling ray made the green feathers on each small back shine like polished jade.

"Oh-h-h! Ah-h-h!" they all cried again.

And then they heard the voice of the sun making a solemn promise.

"The feathers of all hummingbirds will always gleam with this fire-and-jade magic," he said, "so long as they look toward me, face to face. But whenever they turn away from the light, their feathers will darken again to remind them of the gray feathers they first wore—and would still wear if it were not for the unselfish gifts of their new friends."

And so it was on that day when the world was young, and so it has been ever since. When the Great God saw how beautiful these first humming-birds had become, he made other tiny long-billed hummers with radiant hues, giving their feathers all the shining colors of the rainbow, every tint and shade and mixture of red, orange, yellow, green, blue and purple. He asked the sun to give each one his magic fire-and-jewel blessing, and the sun did so gladly. To this day, whenever hummingbirds turn away from the sun's light, some of their shining feathers darken to drab, like fire turning to ashes.

Identified by Ridgway as Spangle Coquette *(Lophornis reginae)*, 1890.

A contemporary view:

If you want to see any hummingbird at its radiant best, you must stand with the light behind you, watching the bird as it faces the sun. The throat and cap feathers, especially the red ones, make an amazing change, turning from red to purple to gray or black, with or without a flash of gold, changing with the changing light. They do so because the red is not true pigment but color borrowed from a ray of light, broken up and reflected by the clear, diamond-like layers of each feather tip.

Under a powerful microscope lens you would see the red throat feathers tipped with tiny, thin layers—very tiny and very thin—each one as clear and colorless as a glass prism and filled with minute air bubbles. Below the clear layers lies a black layer. Each light ray passing through the clear layers is composed of all the colors of the rainbow, and the color reflected depends on how the layers are shaped and tilted and how the light strikes them. All other colors are absorbed by the black layer underneath. If the clear layers do not catch the light ray just right, only the black or a grayish blur comes through for us to see. Only in full sunlight will the red gorget or crown shine like rubies set in gold.

No wonder the Mayas thought these changeable iridescent colors were a magic gift from the sun! And no wonder many other tribes shared the belief, giving these birds such names as Sun Changelings, Flying Sunbeams, Jewels of the Sun, or Tresses of Sun. However, some Navaho storytellers claimed hummingbirds borrowed their colors from the northern lights, while others said the bright hues were taken from flowers or even from the same vari-colored clays that gave the tribe their face paint. Not all tribes, or even all storytellers in the same tribe, explained hummingbird mysteries the same way.

As for the hummer's small size, its use of nectar for food, and its unique flying skill, today's explanation is this: Each bird, each animal of any kind, must fit into its own niche in nature with its own food and habitat and some protection against enemies. The hummingbird size and behavior patterns are those that its niche requires.

Protection for the hummingbird comes in part from its smallness and from its resemblance to bright-hued nectar flowers. A hungry hawk or snake is looking for flesh, not flowers, and so may well pass by a hovering hummer unaware. Legend might call this a magic cloak to make the birds invisible; science terms it camouflage.

When a hummingbird is seen by a predator, it is protected by its superior ability to take off instantly in any direction. Only a very small bird could be airborne so quickly, and only one with strong wing muscles could be so versatile. In proportion to size, the hummingbird breastbone and attached muscles are the most powerful of all birds. Also, the wing structure enables it to gain power on the upstroke as well as downstroke, while other birds can propel themselves only on the downbeat. Wing structure and muscle power also explain why only hummingbirds can hover expertly for so long, as well as fly backward and even upside down for a few brief strokes. Hummingbirds maneuver more like helicopters, while other birds fly more like straight-wing planes. Igor Sikorsky, who invented the helicopter, said he got his best ideas for helicopter design from watching hummingbirds on the wing.

Added protection for females and nestlings comes from the leaf-blending coloring of their backs, and most females lack flashing gorget or crown color to catch a predator's eye. Also, instinct tells a female to build her nest in the shade of a drooping leaf, or elsewhere out of bright sunlight. Her nest, covered with moss or plant fibers, often looks like a natural leaf clump, easily missed by even keen-eyed searchers. Males, with their brighter coloring, are seldom around at nesting time and so don't betray the presence of the nestlings. Both sexes of hummingbirds share the same flying skill and feeding habits, the same wing-whir music that distinguishes this family from all other birds.

II. Why doesn't the hummingbird have a real song?

From the legends of the Navaho people of the North American Southwest:

Long ago when the world was new, birds of field and woods were much alike. All sang much the same twittery song and all were feathered in plain white or gray. Only after a time would some birds earn bright colors or beautiful songs. Only after a time would some be punished for their misdeeds by a change to homely features or harsh voices.

In the beginning, all birds agreed in council that half of them would eat insects, while the other half would eat seeds and berries. In this way, there would be food for all. And they agreed that none of them would eat the flowers. Flowers were to be left alone.

In those long ago days the hummingbird was the same size as the crow. Both had big bodies and big beaks. Both had all-white feathers and both ate only seeds and berries. The hummingbird was the first bird to waken in the morning and he kept eating, eating, eating, all the day, and even in the dusk, for he was always hungry. One day when some other birds scolded him for eating more than his share, he got up still earlier the next morning— so early no one would see him—and went off in secret to eat flowers.

As the hummer nibbled on the petals he made an amazing discovery. The little yellow pollen dust inside each flower cup was both tasty and nourishing. The sweet nectar in each flower was delicious, especially in red, pink or orange blossoms with deep cup shapes. He was so hungry and eager that he ripped the petals apart, leaving them in shreds. He kept ripping petals and sipping nectar and dipping into the pollen till not a flower was left whole. Then he tucked himself under a leaf for a nap.

Shortly other birds came along. They took one look at the shredded flowers and cried aloud in dismay.

"Who did this? Who could be so wicked?"

A striped black-and-yellow butterfly had been poking among the torn blossoms trying to find even one sip of nectar, for nectar is a butterfly's only food. As the birds gathered around her, she lifted her head.

"Don't blame me!" she protested. "My tongue is as dainty as featherdown. I never harm even the smallest petal."

"Then who did this?" demanded the birds.

For answer the butterfly shrugged her wings toward the leaf where the hummer was hiding— and now wide awake. He looked so guilty the birds knew at once he was the culprit.

"I had to do it!" the hummer defended himself. "I was hungry. I'm always hungry. That's the way I am. And I can't help it if I tore the petals with my big beak."

The birds looked at him sternly, then looked at each other. Clearly, something had to be done. If the hummer couldn't help himself, they would have to solve his problem for him.

"If he were not so big," suggested one bird, "he wouldn't need so much food. From now on, let him be the smallest bird of all."

"Yes," another agreed. "And let him have a small beak, too—little and long like a butterfly's tongue."

"Yes! Yes!" chimed all the birds in chorus. In a twinkling the hummingbird began to shrink until his whole body was not even as long as his tail had been. His beak thinned down and stretched out until it looked like a long, thin cactus thorn. His tongue was long and thin, too, and could reach out even beyond the beak tip.

The hummingbird promptly stuck his new, long tongue into a broken flower cup, hoping for a drop of nectar he hadn't been able to reach before. As he lapped it up easily, he was so pleased with himself he opened his beak to sing a ripple of triumph.

But no rippling notes came forth. Only squeaky chirps and twitters. As his body had shrunk, his voice muscles had become so small and twisted that he would never sing again!

He was so dismayed at losing his song that the bluebird—who was always kind and gentle—felt sorry for him. She told the others it was punishment enough to become so small and have such an odd beak. No one had meant for him to lose his song, too. The damage could not be undone, but perhaps there was a way to help.

"Let him have beautiful feathers," she pleaded. "Everyone needs something to be proud of."

No one liked to argue with the kind bluebird, and so it was agreed. To this day the humming-birds have beautiful feathers, but they make more

music with their tiny whirring wings than with
their chittery little voices.

A contemporary view:

Hummingbirds have no real song. Only a few species even
come close, spinning out a little, tinkling tune pleasant
enough to hear, but no rival for the lilting carols of thrushes,
solitaires, wrens, finches, canaries and other feathered song-
sters. Usually, among birds, the males do all or most of the
singing. A male sings first of all to declare which part of the
woods or field or garden is his home territory. The song is
like a musical sign post saying, "This land is mine!" Other
males of his kind will know at once that they should look for
a home elsewhere.

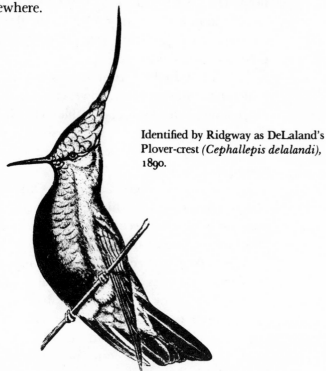

Identified by Ridgway as DeLaland's
Plover-crest *(Cephallepis delalandi),*
1890.

A male sings also to let his mate know he has chosen a
territory and is ready for her to join him, complete the pair
bond and start nesting. While the female is building the nest,
caring for eggs and young, the male's song is her reminder
that this bond between them still holds firm and he is on

guard to protect her and their young. Female birds that sing are usually reaffirming the pair bond, also. However, singing is so much a part of living for most birds, especially in spring-time, that they sometimes sing for no special reason at all, except that they feel like it.

Hummingbirds do not fit this pattern. Instead of claiming their territory with song, they mark out boundaries with chit-tering war cries and dive-bomb attacks on any intruder. They have no need for musical signposts. Also, they court their mates with spectacular displays of flying skill instead of song. Such small birds could scarcely have loud voices, and so the dive-bomb attack and aerial display serve better than would a small, squeaky tune. Furthermore, a song is not needed to reinforce their pair bonding, since that bond is normally broken before nesting begins. Once mating is accomplished, the male is usually off and away to find a new mate elsewhere or to wander where he will.

Occasionally males of a few hummingbird species—espe-cially those living in the tropics on a year-round basis—have been seen sharing nesting duties with their mates, or at least remaining in the general area. In North America only male and female Anna's are together in the same general area year round. Both sexes will roam after nesting season, if food is no longer plentiful, but they do not have the inherited seasonal urge to migrate that sends other species on a regular north-south route each autumn. The male Anna's does not help with the nesting, but he may be attentive to the female for more than just the brief display flights and mating. A male has been seen sitting alongside his mate on the same branch and even feeding from the same flower or syrup container— activities which other hummer species seldom share. Perhaps this behavior is one of the reasons that the Anna's male comes close to having a real song. It is just a thin trill, but it is delivered with flair and fervor and is clearly as much song as he needs.

The Navaho storyteller who first concocted this tale man-aged to weave several answers into one legend. The hum-mingbird's small size and bright colors are accounted for, as well as its lack of a melodious song. Also, a little moral lesson is slipped in to remind listeners that anyone who cannot control himself may have to be disciplined. In order to make that lesson clear, the small size is presented as a punishment. It would surely seem so to most Indians; in their harsh world success usually went to the biggest and strongest. Only occasionally did clever trickery win the day for the small and meek.

Along with the fantasy in this legend is proof that the teller was a keen observer of hummingbird actions. All members of this bird family are indeed early risers—early to rise and late to bed, just like the hummer in the story. This longer day gives them more time for food gathering—and they need it. Hummingbirds must satisfy an almost continual hunger, just like the bird in the story, because they live at a faster pace than other warm-blooded creatures—with faster heartbeats, faster breathing rates and higher body temperatures. They therefore have a greater expenditure of energy than other birds and so need more food in proportion to size.

Experts who study hummer food-gathering habits figure these birds must feed every ten to twelve minutes in order to keep up a normal pace. One White-eared Hummingbird kept captive by Walter Scheithauer in Germany took 267 sips of syrup and ate 677 fruit flies in a sixteen-hour day. This food is burned up so fast that each bird needs to eat about 60-70 percent of its body weight each day for energy renewal. Imagine a 150-pound person having to eat about 90 pounds of food a day!

The tale includes a reminder that butterflies feed on flower nectar, just as hummingbirds do, so this liquid must indeed provide nourishment. No doubt the Navaho listeners of long ago already knew butterfly feeding habits and didn't need to be reminded. They would also have known that both hummingbirds and butterflies find protection in their resemblance to flower petals. If the Navahos hadn't noticed these likenesses, the Omaha people certainly had. The Omaha word for hummingbird means 'bird like a butterfly.'

III. How high and how far can hummingbirds fly?

From the legends of the Paiute Indians of North America's northwestern plains:

In the beginning of time, all animals spoke together, since each understood the speech of every other creature. Each took turns telling what he had seen and learned of how the world is made, so all might gain in wisdom.

The eagle told about snow-capped mountains. The mole told about tunnels underground. The fish told how brook and stream and river all flow down to the ocean. The owl and the bat told of the night. The great, wide-winged white swans told of the cold lands far to the north. And the great, wide-winged black vultures told of the hot lands far to the south. But no one told anything of what might be found up above in the great blue sky spaces, for no one had flown high enough to see their wonders at close range. So the animals decided a bird must be sent to solve this mystery.

The eagle was asked first, since no other bird has better claim to flying power, especially in soaring the heights. But the eagle refused. He said he had nestlings and a mate to care for and would not leave them for such a journey.

The moment he gave his reason, every eye turned to the little cock hummingbird. It was well known he gives his mate no help at all with building the nest or tending the young. And of course it was also known the hummingbirds have strong wings, in spite of their small size.

"When will you start, Little Cock Hummer?" asked the coyote, who was usually the one to speak for all.

"As soon as you provide food for the journey," said Little Cock Hummer.

Immediately the goldfinch suggested he take a lunch of mustard seeds, because they are small, and light and nourishing. All the animals helped to gather the seeds and stuff them into the hummer's feather folds until there was not room for one seed more. Then off he went, up, up, up until no one down on earth could see even a speck in the far blue.

Now it is certainly true that mustard seeds are small and light. And they are doubtless very fine food for goldfinches. But hummingbirds cannot eat seeds of any kind. Little Cock Hummer could neither crack the hard shell nor swallow the seeds whole. So he had no food at all to give him strength for the long upward flight. When he could not go one wing-beat more, he flipped over in a backward somersault and came plummeting back down to earth.

"What did you see? What did you see?" clamored all the animals in chorus. "What is up there beyond the great blue sky spaces?"

At first Little Cock Hummer was too busy gulping down nectar and snatching at passing insects to answer. But finally he spoke.

"Nothing!" he said between gulps. "Up beyond the great blue sky spaces I saw nothing at all!"

"Nothing at all?" gasped the animals in disappointment. They had expected to hear of stars and comets and moonbeams and many other sky wonders.

"Nothing at all!" repeated the hummingbird. "Nothing! Nothing! Nothing!"

And "nothing" was the last word that Little Cock Hummer would ever say on this subject.

From the Mohave tribe of the southwestern United States:
The Mohave people have lived in the sunny southwest lands along the Colorado River for centuries. But in more ancient times when the world was young, so their storytellers always claimed, the tribe lived in some cold, dark place

deep underground.

Food was never plentiful there, and in time it became so scarce that hunger forced them to look for another homeland.

Now and then, a narrow crack opened briefly in the earth-roof over their heads, and they had a glimpse of another world high above their own. It was a land of light instead of darkness, with blue sky and golden sunshine and green growing things that looked good to eat. Each time they had a chance to look through the crack they would sigh and think what a wonderful place that would be for their new home. If only they knew how to get there or had someone to show them the way!

On one day of cold and darkness and hunger, the tribal elders met in council. All agreed only a bird with very strong wings could fly high enough to

reach the crack. And only a very small one could slip through to the world above. The hummingbird was the only bird with these qualifications, so the elders decided to ask his help.

The hummingbird listened politely, then gave a shrug and agreed to go. Off he went on whirring wings to look for a suitable crack. By great good fortune he soon found one. It was just right, with a sturdy grapevine beside it, twining up and up just like a pathway, up, up and through the crack to the world above.

Quickly he flew back and led the Mohave people to the grapevine and pointed out its twisting, twining path. One glimpse and up they went, one after the other, until all were safe in the world above. They have lived in the upper world ever since, and the hummingbird has lived there, too, even though it can fly anywhere it pleases, however high or however far it chooses to go.

A contemporary view:

Even with all the modern equipment to measure time and space, researchers still do not know how high a humming-bird, or any other kind of bird, can fly if it is in the best of health and using the peak of its adult strength. There is no way to exhort a bird—as you would a human—to do its best because the coming flight is for the record. This utmost effort can be called on only when the bird itself realizes the need—as when it must gain height to swoop down on an intruder, to escape a predator, avoid a sudden storm or impress a potential mate of its supreme flying skill.

The answer is further complicated because height is mea-sured two ways. Altitude, in scientific records, is measured as the distance above sea level. But altitude can also refer to the distance between any point in air and the ground below, whether that ground is the tip of a mountain peak or a shore at seaside level. That is how ancient Indians measured it, judging by eye.

Hummingbirds of several kinds — such as the Giant Hummingbird and the Chimborazo Hillstar living in the

Chimborazo Hillstar, by John Gould, London, 1861.

high Andes—nest at twelve to fifteen thousand feet above sea level, while they themselves and their nests may be only a few feet above ground. Many other hummingbird species wing over high mountain passes in the Andes or Rockies on migration, forced to fly at eight to ten thousand feet or more above sea level, yet only fifty to one hundred feet above the ground below. This is normal air-to-ground distance for most small migrants, including hummingbirds. They can fly higher, of course, if they need to avoid storms or other dangers.

Most of the above-sea-level altitude records for birds have come by chance from airplane pilots who happen to catch sight of high-fliers when they have time to identify the species and check the altimeter. Perhaps hummingbirds are too small to have many such readings. Their closest relatives, the swifts, have been recorded flying at a height of seven thousand feet above sea level. That height wouldn't even begin to match the records for hummingbirds in the Andes, and so their final above-sea-level record remains unmarked. However, it will surely belong to some Andean species. In North America, those in the Rockies will win.

How far hummingbirds fly can be measured more easily. Today hundreds of birdwatchers all over the Americas are keeping records of where migrating hummingbirds spend the summer or winter, when they arrive or depart. Even more precise data for all birds is provided by the numbered aluminum leg bands attached under direction of the U.S. Fish and Wildlife Service. The numbers from these bands—or the bands themselves taken from dead birds—are returned to the USFWS (Office of Migratory Bird Management, Laurel, Maryland 20810) and establish records on longevity as well as routes and distances. Plastic leg bands, varied in color to mark year or banding site, can provide similar information at a glance, eliminating the need for capture.

Excellent data on large game birds has been acquired this way. For instance, Snow Geese banded on wintering grounds in California have been found nesting in Siberia. But small non-game birds are less often banded and still less often recovered. The small size of a hummingbird band (1.70 mm inside diameter) makes it difficult to attach and only experts are allowed to handle such an assigment. Consequently, records are few. Bands recovered so far set the average life-span of hummingbirds in the wild at five to eight years; in contrast they live twelve to sixteen years in captivity. This data also records frequent return to former nesting sites but gives us little on distance traveled in migration.

In Colorado, for instance, ten of ninety-two breeding Broad-tailed Hummingbirds banded at the Rocky Mountain Biological Laboratory by Waser and Inouye in 1972-73 were recaptured in the same area a second year, and one a third. Marguerite Baumgartner of Jay, Oklahoma, saw the same Ruby-throated female seven summers out of eight, but none of over one thousand birds banded was re-taken at more than a mile and a half distance. Dan Bystrak of the USFWS Bird Banding Laboratory reported fifty-seven out of seventy-one banded hummers were recovered at the original site, proving a remarkable fidelity to nesting areas but revealing nothing of the distance traveled during migration. The most mileage for those USFWS hummers was 620 miles for a Rufus—not a patch against actual migration distances.

However, mileage checks between verified summer and winter grounds prove the Rufous Hummingbirds fly the farthest of all North American hummingbird species. They normally winter in Mexico and each summer fly north to nesting sites ranging from northern California to Alaska and the Yukon Territory in Canada. The farthest fliers must tally three to four thousand miles each way. Others who stop to nest midway along the Pacific Coast to inland Montana still chalk up close to twenty-five hundred miles on each one-way span.

The Ruby-throated is the only other northern hummer coming close to the records of the Rufous Hummingbird. Ruby-throateds also winter in Mexico, but their flight through eastern United States and Canada is about three thousand miles at the farthest point reported so far. In addition, some Ruby-throateds make a remarkable non-stop flight across the Gulf of Mexico each autumn—five hundred miles with no chance to rest or feed. In the past, many writers insisted these open-water crossings were impossible, because such small birds couldn't store up enough energy for so long a flight. Yet the birds were seen time and again, beyond all doubt. Finally they were also seen feeding heavily before take-off. Before and after checks have now proved they can double their body weight with such gorging, and so arrive in Mexico with energy to spare. Over land, other hummer species have been known to fly non-stop fifteen to twenty hours, followed by a two-week rest to regain weight and strength.

How much Indian storytellers deduced of hummingbird height and distance capabilities cannot now be determined. But both Paiute and Mohave tales show a strong belief in hummer ability to fly high and far. The Mohave tale is only one of several legends from various Southwest tribes claiming their ancestors came in ancient times from a faraway place of cold, darkness and little food. Those who heard the tale in later years, knowing only sunny desert lands, could picture such a place only as some underground world. Today, when research indicates the first Indians in North America came from northern Asia by way of a now-vanished Siberian-Alaskan land bridge, it seems likely this ancient home of cold and darkness was in Alaska. No doubt Rufous Hummingbirds nested there in the past as they do now, migrating southward at the end of their nesting season. So, the legend naming a hummer as the leader of a migration toward warmth and light seems quite reasonable. It is possible that ancient people did indeed follow the hummingbirds southward to a new home.

Many wanderers in the past followed birds across land or water. Columbus, for one, changed course in the autumn of 1492 to follow the piping flocks of migrant shorebirds and so made first landfall in the Bahamas instead of Florida. In a much earlier autumn, the Vikings followed migrating swans southward down European rivers to a warm inland sea and new lands they hadn't known existed.

Swans with their wide, white wings would be easier to see and follow than the smaller, flitting hummingbirds. But a Rufous male with its copper-gold coat and flaming gorget would seem a messenger straight from the gods, a creature of mystery and magic well worth following. Even the female, shining like emeralds, would beckon cold, hungry and discouraged wanderers.

Another hint at the truth behind this fantasy comes from the Navaho belief that hummingbirds got their shining colors from the northern lights. But perhaps imagination alone was enough to give the hummers their role in these stories. After all, no other bird is small and agile enough to slip through the crack in the ceiling of the Navaho mystic netherworld.

The Paiute story seems to have been told to teach a lesson—or perhaps two or three. Perhaps it was told to remind young listeners that any traveler to far places is expected to keep track of what he sees and share it with those at home. Perhaps the storyteller was pointing out that each kind of animal has its own food, and what is good for one may not suit another. Or the real message might have been some Wise One's belief that even the nearest star is farther away than any bird can fly or any human can fathom.

The tales could also express the tribe's uncertainty at how high or how far a small hummingbird can really travel. Today science has to admit much the same lack of knowledge. Also, records are constantly changing. Several species of hummingbirds are steadily expanding their range, flying farther than ever before. Science can point to increasing destruction of their former habitat as the reason for this expansion in today's overcrowded world. But no one can predict how far it will go and whether adaptability to new lands or extinction lies ahead for these adventurers.

IV: How fast can a hummingbird fly?

From the Cherokees of southeastern United States:

When the world was new, birds, other animals and the Cherokee people all lived together. In those long-ago times a hummingbird and a crane were both in love with the same pretty Cherokee maiden. The maiden wished to marry the hummer because he was so handsome, and she thought of a way to get rid of the homely crane without admitting her reason. She declared she would marry whichever one could fly the faster. Of course, she was sure the hummingbird would win.

The other birds were only too ready to set up the race. It was soon decided the course would take them all around the valley's edge and back again in a great circle, starting and ending at the tall pine tree standing beside the maiden's lodge.

The crow appointed himself the starter. "Ready, all ready—GO!" he cawed.

The hummer was off the pine branch in a flash, almost at full speed the moment he lifted his wings. But the crane had to bend his long legs under him and push off even to get moving. When he was finally in mid-air, his wings went at a slow 'fli-i-ip, fla-a-ap' beat. Most of those watching wanted to double their bets on the hummingbird.

The valley was very large, and circling it took more than a day's flight. As the twilight deepened the two racers were still far from their goal. By dark the little hummer was nearly exhausted. He had to stop and sip flower nectar and then take a nap. But he was up and away again long before sunrise, and since he could not see the crane anywhere, he told himself the big, gray fellow was probably still asleep with his head under his wing.

On the hummer went at his usual whirring pace. As he reached the lodge at the circle's end he looked eagerly for the maiden. There she was— with the crane right beside her! The big bird had flown steadily through the night and won the race.

From a Creek legend:
The Creek Indians also seemed sure humming-

birds could be the fastest birds, if only they did not dilly-dally. In their story, too, the race is between a hummingbird and a crane. This time the course was long and roundabout. It began on the banks of a certain winding river and followed every twist and turn, up, up and around until it reached the source high in the hills where the river came bubbling out of the ground.

Of course the hummingbird became hungry after awhile and stopped to sip nectar from the meadow flowers. Then on he went, wings whirring as he followed the river's winding way. But the crane did not stop for food. And he flew high enough to see the hillside spring where the river began, even while he was still far away. Instead of following the winding river, he could fly a straight course and reach the spring long before the hummingbird.

From the Menomini tribe of the land between Lake Michigan and Lake Superior:

Hummingbird portrait engraved by Museum Wormianum, Copenhagen, Denmark, 1655.

Menomini Indians told a tale of a certain medicine maker called Ball Carrier because he possessed a wonderful magic ball he would not give up so long as he had life. One day Ball Carrier learned an evil Spirit Woman had vowed to kill him and take the ball. No sooner had he heard this threat than the Spirit Woman was beside him, ready to make good her challenge.

"We will race," she told him. "The winner will

slay the loser at once and take the ball."

There was no way to refuse, so off they went. The Spirit Woman put all her black magic to work at once and was soon in the lead. So Ball Carrier knew he would have to use magic, too. Quickly he turned himself into the fastest animal he could think of—a long-legged gray wolf. When he still could not catch up he tried other forms—a crow, then a great hawk, a sharp-winged falcon, then a small hawk. Each time the Spirit Woman would overtake him and go ahead.

By this time Ball Carrier was nearly exhausted, but all of a sudden he remembered the fast-whirring wings of the little hummingbird. In a trice he was flying along himself in hummingbird form, going faster and faster until he was only a dazzling gleam in the sunlight. He caught up with the Spirit Woman and passed her easily,for no one, not even an evil spirit, can fly faster than *Na-na-tska,* 'The Hummingbird.'

A contemporary view:

Very likely the Creeks and Cherokees were more interested in teaching a lesson than in proving how fast hummingbirds can fly. They knew every Indian had often watched the hummingbirds and marveled at how fast their wings beat, far faster than the wings of huge long-legged cranes. The story might well have been told as a reminder that 'slow and steady' wins the race if swifter runners stop to eat, sleep or daydream.

The Creek version adds a reminder that a straight line is the shortest distance between two points, and a lofty lookout may save many a weary mile. These bits of wisdom are easily taught, and easily learned, from storytelling.

The Menomini story declares that hummingbirds are the fastest fliers of all—and this is not true. Hummingbirds look as if they fly at great speeds because they are so small. For some reason, most human eyes do not judge speed accurately between two racers of vastly different size. The much smaller body—or machine—always seems to be going faster. Recent statistics collected by Leibowitz for *American Scientist* show that many railroad-crossing accidents occur because the driver of a small car is sure he can drive faster than the approaching train. The same mistake would be made by those watching a hummingbird and a crane. Hummingbirds also seem to be speeding because their wings beat so fast. Watch them as they race and chase across the yard, and their wings are only a blur between blinks. No other bird flies with so fast a wing beat.

Human eyes cannot measure the blur of those wings to count the beats, but electronic devices can. Records now show that hummer wings move from twenty-two beats per second up to a high of ninety per second while hovering. On a plunging courtship dive they may go up to two hundred beats per second! Something like fifty to sixty per second is an average pace on normal flower-to-flower flight.

In comparison, other birds such as chickadees may fly at up to twenty-five wingbeats per second. But, larger birds take far fewer wingbeats. A mockingbird clocks at fourteen beats per second, a common pigeon at five to eight, cranes and herons at only one or two.

Hummingbirds are usually faster at take-off than most birds, too, because their wing structure enables them to gain momentum instantly. It also propels them on both upward and downward strokes, instead of just on the downstroke. But they do not cover distance at the fastest rate. (After all, a four-foot Sandhill Crane with long neck outstretched is already way ahead of a four-inch hummingbird the moment they are in the air.) Hummers can attain twenty-five to thirty miles per hour at their normal speed. In courtship, or while evading an enemy, they may attain fifty to sixty miles per hour. That's faster than most small birds. However, several birds, both large and small, have been timed at more than twice hummer speed. Falcons, eagles, sandpipers, swifts and swallows have all been clocked at over one hundred miles per hour—and even faster in emergencies. Cranes, herons and large waterfowl may do up to seventy miles per hour on migration.

Even if the hummer in these stories hadn't stopped to eat or rest, he wouldn't have won a race with the crane. Provided it is doing its best, the crane is likely to reach the goal first because it can cover the miles faster than the hummer.

The old Indian storytellers were probably not aware of actual speed comparisons, nor were their listeners. They had no instruments to give them such measurements. They could judge only by what they saw, and those fast-beating hummer wings were convincing enough to make the story worth the telling. Even if some Wise One guessed the truth, he might have credited the crane with his victory through steady persistence, a lesson that would serve his listeners well in days ahead. And a good lesson was the reason for many a legend.

Identified by Ridgway as White-booted Racket-tail *(Steganura underwoodi)*, 1890.

v: Which flowers do hummingbirds like best?

From a legend of the Arawak Indians of Venezuela:

One long ago day in a certain Arawak village, three children—a boy and his two little sisters— were waiting patiently for the dreamy-eyed story-teller to look their way.

"Eh, then?" he asked, finally noticing them.

"Please, Wise One," Elder Brother said politely. "We have another question. Which flowers do hummingbirds like best?"

"Hurumph!" the Old One challenged them gruffly. "What answer do your own eyes give you? Do hummers like flowers for their pretty colors, as you do? Or their sweet smell? Or do they have a better reason?"

The little girls looked at each other, waiting for Elder Brother to answer first.

"They like flowers because of the nectar," he said after a moment's thought. "As you have told us, it is their food, given to them by the Great Spirit."

The storyteller nodded. "And so . . . ?"

Elder Brother gulped. "And so I think their favorite flowers are the ones with the most nectar."

"Or the sweetest," his two little sisters answered together.

The storyteller shrugged. "Or perhaps whatever flower is nearest at the moment of hunger?"

"Perhaps," the older girl half agreed, "if they are very hungry. But sometimes they seem to choose favorites. I have watched and watched, and I have seen them go to the pretty pink tobacco flowers first, even when others are closer."

"Ah! Tobacco flowers!" the storyteller said in the kind of voice he used for a special tale. And this is the tale he told...

Long, long ago, the ancient ones of our Arawak tribe had no tobacco growing in their fields. And neither did any other tribe living near us here on these mainland shores beside the sea. Tobacco was grown then only by one tribe and in one place—a sea island not far from here. Our ancestors had always called the island *E-ay-ray*, Land of Hummingbirds, because whenever they went to the island to trade they could see those little glitter-wing birds flitting everywhere. But when the islanders began growing more and more tobacco and offering it for trade, the name changed to Land of Tobacco.

Our ancestors were more than eager to trade for this new and wondrous herb, for the islanders had treated it a special way so it made powerful medicine. They set so high a value on a packet of the dried leaves that our people could never get all they wanted. Other tribes also wanted more than they could match in trade goods. Lest anyone be tempted to steal the plants or seeds and start their own tobacco fields, the islanders set fierce warriors to guard their shores day and night. More than one bold raider tried to slip by these guards and was never seen in his homeland again. One day our Medicine Man gathered the tribal elders together in council, asking if any dared try one more time to steal the tobacco seeds.

As everyone knows, birds and animals and people lived together then, each helping the other. The elders decided a certain wise and crafty Wood Stork should be asked to undertake the task.

The long-legged, big-beaked bird seldom refused a challenge, but this time he shook his homely gray head in refusal. "No, no, do not ask me!" he said. "How could one of my size succeed? The guards would see me before I had a chance to flap a wing. Only someone very small and very fast..."

The moment he said "small" and "fast," both the Wood Stork and the Medicine Man had the same thought.

"The hummingbird!" both exclaimed together. As if in answer, a hummingbird came whirring out of the shadows, its blue-green feathers shimmering like emeralds and sapphires set in gold. Quickly the Medicine man explained the task, and though he warned of certain danger, the little bird was ready to go.

But now the Medicine Man had a new idea. The hummingbird was too small to bring back many seeds. If the Wood Stork went also and hid in the marsh, he could carry home plenty of seeds and the hummingbird, too, if need be.

The Wood Stork agreed, and off the two went.

On *E-ay-ray* the stork hid as he'd been told, but the hummer flew straight to the tobacco fields. He saw hummingbirds everywhere, sipping nectar from the pink tobacco flowers or tending their little moss-cup nests, and he knew he would never be noticed. He darted here and there among the flowers, sipping happily and keeping a sharp lookout for ripe seed pods.

As soon as he found one, he clasped it firmly in his beak and hurried back to tuck it into the stork's feathers and then returned for another. Finally he shoved the last pod into his own feather folds and then off the two birds flew to a heroes' welcome.

The seeds were promptly planted and took firm root. Ever since that long-ago day we Arawaks have grown our own tobacco while hummingbirds watch over our fields keeping the crop safe from harm and sipping the nectar as their reward.

You may indeed name the tobacco flowers among the hummingbird's favorites. If you want to know the others—let your own eyes tell you!

A contemporary view:

The Arawak tale contains more than a twist of truth. Hummingbirds do indeed visit tobacco flowers often, both in farm fields and flower gardens. Anyone who watches hummingbirds long enough—and in places where flowers of many kinds bloom—will observe that their favorites are often similar to tobacco flowers with a tubelike form and bright colors, especially pink, red and orange. The tube or trumpet shape provides more room for nectar than an open-faced flower, so the birds soon recognize it as a promise of rich feeding. Experience also teaches them that pink, red and orange flowers are most likely to hold sweet nectar. So, they try these flowers first. But they will sip from flowers of any shape or color when they are hungry—and return to them again if the nectar is sweet and plentiful.

Hummingbird food must be sweet—and therefore rich in energy-giving carbohydrates—to keep the birds flying at their fast pace. Nectar is not just a sweet treat for them, it is life itself. For added nourishment they also feed on pollen, rich in muscle-building protein, and they obtain still more protein from insects, at the same time devouring pests that harm the tobacco and other plants. They hunt insects in the flower cups or in mid-air, darting into a swarm of tiny 'no-see-ums' like ballerinas dancing on their tails instead of their toes.

Perhaps the Medicine Man who first told this tale knew some flowers hold more nectar than others, perhaps not. But he certainly knew that the Arawaks of the South American mainland had taken their first cultivated tobacco in a raid on *E-ay-ray*, Land of Hummingbirds, and that hummers and tobacco had long been linked in tribal lore. Doubtless he knew from his own observation that the plants reproduced better when hummingbirds were plentiful. Evidence indicates several tribes knew the birds aided reproduction by transferring pollen from plant to plant. He may have counted it magic, instead of realizing that some plants reproduce sexually, with pollen having the role of male sperm. But at least he recognized the crucial link joining hummingbirds, pollen and good crops.

Tobacco became the First Medicine for the Arawaks, highly valued for its healing power and magic. Because hummingbirds had a share in its propagation, the little birds were paid full tribute in tribal culture. Soon they were known to many as Tobacco Bringers, Medicine Birds, Doctor Birds or Birds of Magic.

Today, tobacco is not considered medicine. It is used for pleasure, even though the surgeon-general of the United States and many other physicians have tested its effect on the human body and declared it injurious to health. But to the Indians of old its goodness was unquestioned, and in the early years of American exploration and settlement many pioneers counted it good medicine also, accepting the Indians' advice. Actually, it does have medicinal value. A poultice of tobacco will ease the soreness of a toothache or open wound. Also, blowing smoke into a throbbing ear will relieve the pain through its penetrating warmth. Today other remedies are available for these ills, but in the past tobacco was a boon and much respected.

Colonists from Europe began calling the hummingbirds Doctor Birds, too—and that name is still heard in Caribbean lands to this day. (See Chapter 8 for species.) In most areas it is applied to one species in particular. On Tobago, for instance, it is the Rufous-breasted Hermit. On the coast of Venezuela where this Arawak tale is still heard, the term belongs to a species officially known now as the Copper-rumped Hummingbird, and its Latin label of *Amazilia tobaci* (tobacco bird from Amazon country) hints it may indeed be the bird of legend.

The island of *E-ay-ray* is now Trinidad, the name bestowed by Christopher Columbus on his third voyage to the Caribbean in the summer of 1498. Tobacco was still an important crop there, and for more than a century it was known to many Europeans as *trinidado*. The Spaniards were already using the word *tabaco*, borrowed from the Taino Indians as the name for this New World plant, and the English 'tobacco' soon followed.

The legendary link between hummingbirds and tobacco has a factual counterpart in the real bond between hummingbirds and vanilla. Vanilla vines, like tobacco plants, originally grew only in the New World. Both were used by American Indians long before Europeans arrived, and both, for a time, were cultivated as a crop only in only one place.

First picture of a tobacco plant in English print, trans. by John Frampton, London, 1577.

In 1519 when the Spaniards invaded Mexico under Hernan Cortes and his conquistadores, vanilla was raised only in the southeastern lands ruled by the Aztecs. The Spaniards made it their monopoly, too, and refused to sell seeds or cuttings to rival Europeans who might use them to start their own vanilla plantations elsewhere. Both Spaniards and Mexicans guarded the secret of how the seed pods were dried in sun and shade to bring out the wonderful vanilla flavor, and how the vines were planted and tended so they would flourish.

For three hundred years the secrets were well kept, and the price of vanilla remained high. Then in 1829 some French planters finally got hold of some cuttings and smuggled them off to a French-owned island named Bourbon in the Indian Ocean. There the soil and climate were much the same as in Mexico and the cuttings rooted and grew well. In time the vines produced the lovely tube-shaped, yellow-green flowers; but seed pods never formed! And that was a disaster, since only the pods and beanlike seeds yield the vanilla flavor.

The French planters were devastated. They could not even begin to guess what had gone wrong. But they had invested too much in the project to give up easily, and they finally met someone from Mexico who explained to them that vanilla flowers cannot pollinate themselves. The stamen and pistil are not placed so pollination can easily take place. In Mexico, the pollen is transferred from stamen to pistil only by a certain tiny bee and by hummingbirds reaching in for nectar with their long bills and tongues. Both bees and hummingbirds are found only in the Americas. Therefore the French planters on Bourbon had to figure out a way to transfer the pollen themselves—by hand. This had to be done with a very delicate touch or the flowers would be ruined. Several attempts failed, but the French finally solved the problem by using a splinter of bamboo about the size and shape of a hummingbird beak.

By the time this bond between hummingbirds and vanilla was well known, most people were talking more of science than of magic. The name Vanilla Bird has not persisted as Doctor Bird and Tobacco Bird have. Nevertheless, the vanilla flower, a member of the orchid family, would have been recognized as a favorite hummingbird blossom to all who used their own eyes as the Arawak storyteller suggested.

From the Carib and Warrau, neighbors on the Caribbean's South American shores:

Both Carib and Warrau tribes honored the hummingbird as Tobacco Bringer. In their tales, too, the little raider was usually accompanied by some larger, long-legged bird—crane, wood stork or heron.

Sometimes the Long-legs was a vain creature who wanted all the glory for himself, even though the hummer did all the work. He tried to trick the little one and leave it behind on *E-ay-ray*, or at least get a head start and reach home long before the hummer's small wings could carry him in pursuit. But the hummer was always able to put on an amazing burst of speed and reach home first. The hummer reputation for swiftness was part of this version, too.

Some storytellers also added lessons in perseverance, in admitting mistakes and trying again. In their tale the hummingbird went alone and foolishly brought back only flowers, forgetting that seeds for planting, not just nectar for his own pleasure, were needed. Once told of his mistake, the hummer resolutely went back for the seeds and so won honor and his name as Tobacco Bringer.

It seems likely some who remembered this version when they themselves had need to try again after failure, would think of hummingbirds with a very special affection.

From the Cherokees of North America:

Far to northward, in what is now the southeastern United States, the Cherokee people also knew the hummingbird as Tobacco Bringer. These tales revealed that the Cherokees had once been able to gather all the tobacco they needed from wild plants growing in their own lands. They used it for medicine and for certain sacred ceremonies and never thought a day would come when no wild tobacco could be found.

In some versions, tobacco vanished because a wicked wild goose carried it off to some faraway stronghold in the southland. In others, the storyteller simply admitted the wild plants had been used up with no thought of need for re-planting. At any rate, no tobacco could be found and the people missed it sorely, especially when their beloved Elder fell ill and only tobacco would ease the suffering.

Many a brave Cherokee started on the long southward journey to obtain this medicine, but none ever returned. Finally a little hummingbird (or, in some versions, a Medicine Man who could turn himself into a hummingbird) volunteered to go. Of course he was successful, and was no sooner home again with the precious leaves—and some seeds for planting, too—than the Elder inhaled the smoke and recovered.

The bird of the Cherokee legends has to be the Ruby-throated Hummingbird, for it is the only species nesting in eastern North America.

From the Chayma people of Trinidad:

In the days of the Chayma, the island was indeed a land of hummingbirds. This tribe believed the jewel-toned birds were the souls of long-dead tribal ancestors. Hummingbirds were therefore held sacred, and the people made sure the tobacco their ancestors had cherished in life would be well tended so the spirit birds could enjoy it also. Anyone who harmed the little birds was sure to incur the wrath of the gods.

For ages the Chayma people had obeyed this tabu. Other birds were slain for feather ornaments or food, but never the hummingbirds. Then one day a fierce war party of cannibals invaded the island and the Chayma warriors sprang to attack in such frenzy that, for once, the cannibals retreated without a single victim.

The Chaymas were so elated they forgot everything except the victory celebration and the feather headdresses and cloaks each warrior must wear.

They began killing every bird in sight, even the sacred hummingbird, the tabu forgotten.

But the gods did not forget. No sooner did the feather-clad dancers take their place in a circle, than the earth began to tremble beneath their feet and great spouts of boiling black tar came welling up in their midst, sucking them down into the rumbling, odorous depths, never to be seen again. Though the people vanished, the tar pit remains as everlasting reminder of the vengeance of the gods if hummingbirds are not protected.

A contemporary view:

Scientists suggest the sudden upwelling of tar did indeed occur, caused by some natural change beneath the earth's surface, such as an earthquake. Chayma storytellers of later years may have understood this very well, but repeated the legend as the best way to save hummingbirds from extinction. Whether they did so for the sake of the birds themselves, or to maintain their own power through preserving the ancient fear of spirit vengeance, cannot be known.

Other tribes also tried to control hummingbird survival by

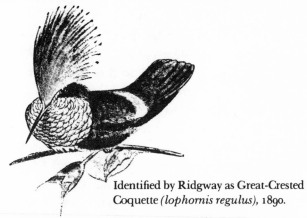

Identified by Ridgway as Great-Crested Coquette *(lophornis regulus)*, 1890.

limiting the use of their ornamental feathers to chieftains and nobles. Of course, nobility in any culture has always claimed its privileges. But hummingbirds are so small that hundreds would have to be slain to make a single cloak, and the danger of overkill resulting in extinction was very real.

On a small island such as *E-ay-ray*, the threat is greater than on mainland shores, for there is no surplus population nearby to replace those killed. Chayma Wise Ones may have realized this danger and seized upon the sudden eruption of the tar lake as a warning not easily forgotten. Whether the legend helped or not, *E-ay-ray* is still a 'Land of Hummingbirds,' even now when it is called Trinidad. The Asa Wright Nature Centre there—some two hundred acres of forested mountain land—is home to twelve different species.

VI: Why are hummingbirds called rain birds?

From the Pima tribe of southwestern United States:

In the days of the Ancient Ones, the whole of Pima country knew a summer of terrible heat. Not a drop of rain fell. Not a breath of wind stirred. Somehow, the Pima people had angered both the Rain Spirit and the Wind Spirit, and the two had taken themselves off to a hiding place in the mountains, vowing never to return.

All the Pima prayers, their sacred songs and dances, counted for nothing. The two haughty spirits stayed in their secret cave, giving no heed to Pima pleas. Day after day the air was still and windless. Beans dried on the vines. Corn and chili peppers shriveled on their stems. And all in Pima land knew they would soon die, too—man and bird and beast—if no rain came.

In despair the Pima Wise Man begged the bravest men and strongest creatures among them to find those two angry spirits and persuade them to return. Many a man and many a willing creature did his utmost, but none could find the hiding place. Once again the Wise Man called a council, asking the same troubled question, meeting the same troubled silence for answer.

Suddenly a little hummingbird spoke up. "Let me try. If..."

"You!" interrupted several voices in scorn.

"What can a little thing like you do?"

The hummer said, "Give me a braided thong, no wider than this tongue of mine and made from the hair of your chieftain's daughter, then you will see what I can do."

The maiden cut some of her hair and braided it into a black and silken thong, and off the hummer went.

The hummingbird had a certain magic white feather in his tail. The moment he took to the air, this white feather would point to windward. So all he had to do was fly where the white feather pointed and he would find the Wind Spirit. Of course, the Rain Spirit would be with him. The hummer flew as his magic feather directed and soon found the cave where the spirits slept side by side.

Quickly he twisted the magic thong around them, tying the last knot just as they wakened. He told them of his magic and threatened they would be prisoners forever unless they promised to return to Pima country. The spirits had no choice but to agree, and so the hummer led them back to the waiting tribe, pledging he himself would make sure the promises were kept. Ever since, the rain, the wind and the hummingbirds have all been coming to Pima lands at the same time.

A contemporary view:

Rain and hummingbirds often appear together, especially in the Southwest. In these hot lands, most flowers bloom only when it rains, and then lie dormant until rain comes again. Since hummingbirds can live only where flowers bloom to yield pollen and nectar, they usually appear only in the rainy season. When hot dry weather bleaches the valleys, leaving flowers dead and dying, hummingbirds move up to cooler hillsides where the blossoms are still fresh and sweet. When rains return to the valleys, flowers return and so do the hummingbirds. Often rains, flowers and hummingbirds arrive so nearly all at once that a storyteller would easily be tempted to make up a tale explaining which brings the others.

All observers, even those without a storyteller's imagination, can see that hummingbirds seem to enjoy the rain, accepting it almost as if it were their tribute. They flit and flash through the gently falling drops, taking a showerbath on the wing. Or they sit on a bare branch, ruffling their feathers this way and that until they are wet right down to the skin. Even after the rain stops, they still seek out some cupped leaf for an elf-size bathtub to continue their soaking. Such bathing on the wing or in a leaf tub is the only way they get a good splashing because the ordinary mudpuddle or stream or backyard birdbath is too deep for their midget size.

In the desert, a gentle rain could easily seem a gift of Nature meant especially for hummingbirds and reason enough for any southwest tribe to give them the Rain Bird title. Whether the Pimas thought of all hummingbirds as Rain Birds, or gave the title to only one species is not easy to decide now. The fact that the storyteller spoke of a bird with white tail feathers seems to point to just one species. However, the females of nine out of ten hummingbird species usually seen in this area today have white-tipped tail feathers. In just one species—the Blue-throated Hummingbird—do both males and females flaunt the easily-seen white tail corners. Consequently the Blue-throated cock may have the strongest claim to legendary honors, since the storytellers spoke of the magic bird as a male.

In Mexico, however, tradition points to another species, the Broad-billed Hummingbird. Evidently this hummer's rattling quills, heard so often in the rainy season, were the first to suggest to ancient Medicine Men that a similar rattling sound incorporated into their ceremonial dance might bring the hoped-for rain. Dried seeds inside a gourd produced the imitative rattle, and the Broad-billed's Spanish name *Matraquita*, meaning 'Little Rattle-Shaker,' keeps the old belief alive.

From the Hopi, Zuñi and other Pueblo groups of the Southwest:

All tribes in the arid Southwest shared the Pimas' reasons for believing hummingbirds might intercede with the gods to bring needed rain. Almost any bird with wings to carry it up to the sky realms where the gods were thought to dwell might have this role. However, the hummingbirds' connection with the rain and the blossoming of the desert gave them special rank. Painting their likeness on a water jar was one way of asking their help in bringing the rain to keep the jars well filled. Numerous Pueblo jars in museum collections feature a Rain Bird motif, some too abstract in form to identify easily as hummingbirds, but others with more than a hint of realism.

Zia Rain Bird from water jar.

The ancient Nazca people of Peru's coastal desert may have shared similar ideas about the connection between hummingbirds and rain. They sometimes pictured hummingbirds on their water jars, too.

Peruvian water jar, in Linden Museum, Stuttgart.

Hopi and Zuñi tribes gave the hummingbird a definite place as Rain Bringer in their ceremonial dances. For both tribes, the dancers represented spirits known as *kachinas* and wore masks and costumes to identify the bird or animal they portrayed. Both the hummingbird itself and its *kachina* were known as *Tocha* to the Hopis and *Tanya* to the Zuñis and both names seem to stem from the word for 'bee.'

A long bill and a few feathers—as well as the traditional mask to hide the dancer's identity—are all *kachinas* need to look like a hummingbird. However, costumes for special ceremonies could be much more elaborate, calling for turquoise and silver necklaces, bracelets, rings and fancy knee-length kilts of softest leather and swishing fox-tail trim, a circlet of jingling bells below each knee, and more bells and tassels on calf-high boots as well as a larger-than-life image of a hummingbird atop the helmet mask.

But there was no such splendor for the two little *Tocha* dancers at a Hopi planting festival on February 1, 1900. The government ethnologist privileged to view the dance sketched them for his report as barefooted with only a scant loin-cloth covering, a twist of blue yarn below each knee and a row of fluttering green feathers glued to each arm. Each wore a helmet mask made out of a hollowed gourd painted blue, with an appropriate long bill inserted between the eye-holes. Their naked bodies were painted yellow on the front and green on the back. In spite of such minor disguise, they whirled and twirled and whirled again, liveliest—and smallest—of the *kachina* dancers.

Hopi *Kachina* dancers, U.S. Bureau of Anthropology, 1900.

They were also among the best beloved in Hopi villages. When miniature *kachina* figures were given to the children after the ceremony—not as toys but as reminders of tribal traditions—*Tocha kachinas* were always among those most highly prized.

Rain Birds and flood legends of Pima and Michoacán:

Pima Indians and the Michoacáns of Mexico are among the many tribes with legends of an ancient torrential downpour bringing devastating floods. In these tales, as in the Bible story of the great flood (Genesis 8:8-12), a good and kindly man took birds and beasts aboard his boat to save them from the raging waters. In the Bible, Noah looked out from his Ark as the waters finally receded and sent forth a raven to learn if there were once more good firm land where he might come to anchor. When the raven did not return, he sent out a dove. In the Indian tales, the first bird sent forth was a vulture, and when it did not return, a hummingbird was chosen as a more reliable messenger. Very shortly, the hummingbird—like Noah's dove—returned with a green leaf or flower as proof the earth could once more be a safe home.

In the Pima tale, the Great Spirit then commanded the hummingbird to work with the coyote in bringing him damp clay from beneath the waters so he might fashion more men and women to inhabit the earth. The hummer did so, giving those who believed the legend a prime reason to call the hummer a Life Giver and to hold it sacred.

Like the Chaymas on *E-ay-ray,* the Pimas believed these smallest birds were not to be killed for food or feathers. They warned all the tribe that if anyone harmed a hummingbird, the flood waters would return full force, sweeping all to destruction. Any hummingbird killed by mischance was to be buried with fitting ceremony, and gifts for the Great Spirit were to be placed on its grave in penitent token. Even to this day when a flood comes to Pima country, someone is almost sure to ask who has been molesting the hummingbirds.

Rain Bird beliefs from the Toltecs:

Toltec Indians of Mexico also respected the

hummingbird as Rain Bringer, an identity shared by both a mythical warrior and a spirit-being. Their name for bird or warrior was *tozcatl*. The spirit-being in hummingbird form was *tozcatlpoca*, with the suffix meaning 'wizard,' 'sorcerer' or 'magic maker.'

Aztec rain dancers, from Fray Diego Duran, 1597.

To them *tozcatl* meant both 'rain bringer' and 'life bringer.' The double usage was quite reasonable, for renewed rain means renewed life for all growing things in these hot and arid lands where drought seasons and rainy seasons alternate in a regular pattern, year after year. Hummingbirds were also Life Bringers because of their role in transferring pollen from plant to plant, thereby insuring the production of flower, fruit and seed. Many early tribes in the Southwest understood pollen's importance, as their names for this golden powder prove, and the Toltecs were evidently among this group. Even without a surviving legend to explain how the hummingbird came by this rain-bringing, life-bringing power, the name alone indicates tribal reverence.

A contemporary view:

When flowers and insects die in an unexpected cold snap, hummingbirds are suddenly left without food. Their bodies react to solve this cold-and-hunger crisis in a remarkable way. Instead of dashing about wasting energy in a useless search for food, the birds settle into some protected nook and within a few hours drop into a sleeplike torpor so deep it seems like death. All physical functions are dramatically reduced—lower body temperature, heart beat, oxygen consumption and breathing rate—and in this state the birds have little need for warmth and food.

In the tropics, semi-tropics and temperate-zone summers that hummingbirds know, such severe cold usually ends in a few hours with warm rains that bring opening buds and newly hatched insects. Hummingbirds then rouse from their torpor with a completeness that seemed a miraculous return

Identified by Ridgway as Allied Emerald
(Agyrtria Affinis), 1890.

from death to ancient Indians and gave added reason for linking hummingbirds with rain and life-force in tribal lore.

Certain mammals in temperate zones go into a similar cold-weather trance that lasts an entire three-month winter. Their torpor is called hibernation, a term formed from the Latin word for 'winter period.' The hummingbird reaction needs a different label because hummers enter this stage more briefly and at any time of year, night or day, as need arises. The term most often used by scientists is torpidation, meaning 'stiff and numb period.'

Just how long hummers can maintain torpor and still return to active life is a question not yet fully answered. One test recorded by Pearson in 1969 described a hummer that began to lower body temperature and oxygen consumption within twenty minutes after going to night roost, was in complete torpor by midnight and did not rouse until after sunrise. Probably most hummingbirds torpidate for some period during a cold night. Those in high altitudes or colder temperate areas may need to do so every night and sometimes by day also. The effective period could be extended over several days instead of twelve or more hours if the birds can rouse briefly to feed from a backyard syrup container or whatever natural food has survived the frost, then return to torpor. Laboratory tests reported by Hainsworth and Wolf for *Science* in 1970 showed that some northern species can hold torpor longer and at colder air temperatures than tropical species. Almost certainly the species that live in colder areas and so are forced into torpidation most often will develop the greatest skill in maintaining this life-saving reaction.

Hummingbirds living in the high Andes must be among the experts. The Anna's Hummingbird, living year round in western North America, has also proven proficient in laboratory tests. Few birds of other families have been tested on this point. But swifts torpidate regularly. Nightjars may also, for the Common Poorwill in southwest mountain areas actually hibernates, remaining in winter torpidity eighty-eight days or more, a behavior well known to Hopi Indians who long ago named it *holchko* (the sleeper). Chickadees also torpidate briefly on a cold winter night, and some ornithologists believe that all small birds—who have the least room for storing surplus fat—can torpidate to some extent. Much more study is needed on this subject, but it has long been a fact of hummingbird behavior persistently confused with fantasy.

Another fact-or-fantasy conflict has clung to the hummingbird's sudden change of colors. Optical science explains the change is due to shifts in the angle of refracted light reflected from the hummers' feathers, but to the people of older times only magic could be responsible. And since such powers seldom come singly, all kinds of wonders became linked with hummmer lore and legend.

Biloxi-Sioux Indians claimed if you could get a hummingbird to answer your questions, it would always tell the truth. The Aztecs wore a circlet of hummingbird feathers as a love charm that never failed, and the wearer also gained good luck at games of chance.

Early North American pioneers of European ancestry added to the folklore, spreading the story that if a hummingbird chanced to alight on your hand or arm or head, you would soon be wealthy enough to wear jewels and silken finery as beautiful as the bird's own plumage.

In lore and legend the hummingbird bridges the time span from ancient to modern, from Giver of Life to Giver of Luck. And even in this prosaic era of the computer, there are still plenty of people who consider seeing a hummingbird part of any day's good fortune.

VII: Why are hummingbirds always fighting each other?

From the legends of the Aztecs of Mexico:

> Once in the long, long ago, the Aztecs were a nomad tribe wandering south into Mexico in search of a homeland where the sun would be warm and the mountain breezes cool. Led by a valiant warrior named *Huitzitzil*, they found just such a place and began to build their city.
>
> But nearby tribes coveted this place, too, and

came swarming down to drive the Aztecs away. With *Huitzitzil* at their head, the Aztecs fought bravely, marveling at his skill with a sharp-pointed spear. One by one, the attackers gave way, and just as the last enemy fighters were about to turn and run, an arrow came zinging through the air and pierced *Huitzitzil* through the heart, killing him instantly.

Many Aztec warriors saw their leader fall. But they could not turn back to aid him, for the enemy now took courage and began to rally. The Aztecs rushed to renew attack, shouting their war cries and curses, and at last could count themselves victors. As they hastened to look for their hero's body, they discovered it had vanished! Suddenly a green-coated hummingbird came whirring up from the very spot where *Huitzitzil* had fallen. And the Aztecs knew at once that this bird was their hero's spirit.

No doubt entered their minds, since *Huitzitzil* means 'Shining One with the Weapon,' a perfect description of both their hero and the bird that wielded its long beak like a warrior's spear. Too, *Huitzitzil* had always worn a circlet of shining hummingbird feathers on his left wrist, showing his reverence for the bird whose name he shared.

They gazed in awe at the little bird, wondering if their hero had come from the spirit world in the beginning, taking man-shape for just a time in order to lead them to a new home. Or had he been a man and now was turned into a spirit bird as reward from the gods for his bravery?

At any rate, they were certain their hero now had magic power beyond human reckoning and could be called *pochtli,* a sorcerer, wizard or worker of magic. *Huitzitzilopochtli* became his name and the Aztecs revered him as their war god. When they learned that the Toltecs — their conquered enemy— also had a hummingbird wizard god, *Tozcatlpoca*, its statue was brought to stand beside the image of *Huitzitzilopochtli* in the temple.

In time, the Aztecs came to believe that every one of their warriors who died in battle would be turned into a hummingbird. At first, each warrior-turned-hummer would be granted a time of ease in the flower-filled gardens of paradise, with sweet nectar for their daily food. At need, each would become a soldier again, in hummingbird form, part of a wizard-warrior band led by *Huitzitzilo-pochtli*.

Aztec hummingbird dancer *(Huitzilopochtli)*, from Fray Diego Duran, 1579.

By day these wizard warriors were ordered to roam the fields, living on nectar as they had in paradise. As they roamed, they were to sharpen their skills with mock attack on every humming-bird they met—or on any other bird they wished to confront. They were warned to keep ever ready for battle, because each evening at dusk *Huitzitzilo-*

pochtli would call on them to help fight off the evil powers of darkness. Without this nightly defense, darkness might envelop the earth for all time, depriving the world of the sun's warmth and golden light. As soon as the darkness gave first sign of weakening, as it did each dawning, the hummer warriors were to rally again for a battle to ensure the sun's appearance in full glory.

At certain times of year, as everyone knew, the powers of darkness were stronger than usual, enabling the shadows of night to remain longer. This was the season when the wizard warriors would have to fight harder and longer, if the sun were to return. They pledged to give all they had of strength and courage and skill for the sun's sake. In turn, the sun gave them due reward, for whenever the hummingbirds face the sun, their feathers are touched with its golden radiance and their throat feathers glow like precious jewels set in gold.

To aid the wizard warriors in this dark-of-the-year battle, the Aztecs would hold a special ceremonial dance. The ritual began at noon, when the sun was highest and brightest. The dancers were youths and maidens from noble families, well-trained by temple dancing masters. Joining hands in a circle, round and round they danced, keeping time with graceful steps to the music of tootling pipes and thumping drums. At a signal note they stopped short, each lifting a hand high, and then begain chanting the song of *Huitzitzilo-pochtli:*

> I am the Shining One—bird, warrior and wizard. I have no equal—no, not even one. Never in vain do I wage nightly battle. For mine is the magic that brings back the sun!

Then the watchers saw each youth turn to the girl on his left and, with both hands at her waist, lift her high as if she were a hummingbird in whirring flight—and the dance was done. No one ever doubted that the dancers—and the hummingbirds themselves, *Huitzitzilopochtli's* wizard warriors—worked their magic, for the sun always returned.

Aztec dancers, from Fray Diego Duran, 1579.

A contemporary view:

The Aztec legend must have been easy to believe. Anyone watching hummingbirds can see how they attack each other—or any other intruder—at headlong tilt, chittering and chasing. At times, a bird will belabor some rival with its beak as if it were a war club or spear, slashing away with whacking, thwacking blows. These 'wizard warriors' are most active at dawn and dusk, among the earliest birds on the wing each morning and the last to flutter past in the almost-dark.

Hummers have to defend their feeding territory so fiercely and over such a long day because they need more food—in proportion to their body size—than other birds. Keeping the territory for themselves and remaining active over a longer day is the only way they can obtain all the food they need. Larger animals have body room to store large amounts of fat to be burned as fuel when needed. But hummingbirds have scant room on their tiny frames. When food is scarce, they survive by keeping it all for themselves—not in greed but in simple need for survival.

Hummingbirds do not arrive at this knowledge by reasoning. They are born to this pattern and they follow it. If food supply is ample, they may allow others to feed with them in peace, or at least in a temporary truce. Lucky watchers may see a dozen hummers—even as many as fifty if the feeding is lush—all sipping from the same flower-laden branches of some locust or madrona tree, a buddleia bush or a tempting row of fuchsia baskets.

Even amid such plenty, some individuals may still be ready for battle, especially at dusk when they are most driven to stoke up their bodies for the night. Again in the morning, when energy is lowest, or after a long migration journey, their belligerence may be excessive. We can watch them now and understand, but the Aztecs watched in awed wonder—and firm belief in magic.

From the Nez Perce of the North American West:

The Nez Perce people, who once lived in the chimney-corner of Idaho, told a tale picturing the hummingbirds as spirits of certain folk who in life had been selfish and mean-tempered. In particular, there were two greedy-minded brothers who could take the form of humans or hummingbirds as they pleased, or as some magic power decreed. They lived in Lochsa Canyon at the very headwaters of the Lochsa River, and whether they were in the guise of birds of humans, they never let anyone else cross their land. Whoever dared trespass was promptly beheaded and his skull turned into solid rock.

One day the coyote, with the help of a clever magpie, tricked the two brothers into thinking he was weak and beyond a fight. The moment the brothers turned away, the coyote killed them and turned them both to stone. Everyone roundabout was delighted, because now they could cross the canyon without a fight. To this day you can still see the two stones where the coyote left them as warning and reminder.

From the Kwakiutl:

Farther west than Nez Perce country, the Kwakiutl people made their home beside Pacific shores. They also had noted the belligerent ways of most hummingbirds and of one hummingbird in particular who staked out its claim beside a stream where the Kwakiutls liked to bathe.

When this hummingbird was around, the people had to bathe elsewhere or run the risk of attack. Just let them step too close to some invisible line and the bird would come swooping down from its perch, beak poised for jabbing, stabbing blows—sometimes sharp enough to draw blood.

Whether this tale was told to shame some listener for his selfishness is not certain. It could just as easily have been intended as a good example of the way a person should defend his own home and village from attack.

From the Navahos:

For the most part, tales of hummingbird belligerence were told with respect and admiration for its boldness and audacity. The Navahos, for instance, paid the hummingbirds special honor for both swiftness and courage. For them it was one of the four bravest creatures they knew, a spirit-being who in some distant past had served Navaho people well. In that ancient time, the Navahos were in great need of food, and four spirit-creatures set out to obtain it at whatever cost might be demanded by long and arduous journey.

Corn was the food these four brave ones brought back to the Navahos. The wolf, who went first, returned with white corn. The mountain lion brought yellow corn. The bluebird came with blue corn, as might be expected. And the hummingbird returned with an ear of corn showing kernels of every hue—red, white, blue and yellow. These were the colors of its own bright feathers, of course, and also of the northern lights. Whenever these lights could be seen on a winter night, some Navaho storyteller was sure to point them out with awe and wonder and another telling of the hummingbird's long journey to a mystic land.

This hummingbird corn-of-many-colors still grows in fields where the plants are allowed to develop in their own ancient way. They are often sold in city markets for autumn holiday decorations, but few who buy them know the old Navaho tale matching their colors to the jewel-bright hues of hummingbirds. Such a story may be only the briefest criss-cross of threads in the multiplex weavings of Indian nature lore, but—like all the others—it is well worth the written records that keep old traditions in memory.

4.

FIRST WRITTEN RECORDS

IN THE EARLY years of New World exploration, many a startled European glimpsed his first hummingbird without having the least hint such tiny, jewel-feathered hoverers existed. One good look at the little whir-wings and scholar, churchman, soldier, sailor, colonist and adventurer were all equally eager to send back written word of these just-discovered marvels.

Pen in hand, they were suddenly halted by a troublesome question: What do you call a bird unlike any known in Europe? Do you just make up a name in your own language? Or must you use scholar's Latin? Or could you borrow an

Indian name—and if you did, how difficult would it be to match the strange-sounding spoken syllables with written letters?

One way or another, decisions were made and written names and descriptions of this New World discovery began appearing in European letters, travel diaries and official reports. Quite reasonably, the Spaniards were first with written records of this small bird as they had been with all written accounts of New World exploration, but others soon followed.

SPANISH, ITALIAN AND PORTUGUESE

Christopher Columbus, who first saw the Caribbean islands he called "The Indies" in the autumn of 1492, was almost certainly the first European to make written mention of hummingbirds. Although he made no detailed description for positive identification, his journal entry for October 21, 1492, gives a strong hint he had just glimpsed this New World wonder. "Little birds," he wrote, "... so different from ours it is a marvel."

Someone who followed Columbus to the Indies on later voyages—or Columbus himself—must have supplied further details. At least the surprising smallness of these birds was known to Pietro Martire de Anghiera, the Italian scholar who served Queen Isabella as valued diplomatic envoy and tutor to young court pages. As a member of Isabella and Ferdinand's court, he had access to every report and trophy from returned voyagers and was fascinated with their discoveries.

He became thoroughly Spanish in loyalties, even changed his name to its Spanish equivalent, Pedro Martir de Angleria. However, he continued to write numerous letters to scholarly friends and former benefactors back in Italy, especially when he could relate stories of the Indies lands he himself first called the New World. Back in Italy his letters were passed from hand to hand and marveled over, even in the Vatican. Some were published in Italy without his consent. Others he published in Spain, among them one noting the presence in the Indies of little birds even tinier than the ones Italians called *regolo* (kinglet).

For Italians, this one word named any of three species now known as Goldcrest, Willow Warbler and Winter Wren. The French called them all kinglets, too—*roitelets*—while the English knew the three as wrens. Whatever their names, the birds were all of the same 3½- to 4-inch size and known throughout Europe as the smallest birds in the world. Mention of birds still smaller was cause for wonder indeed, and Angleria's letter was bound to stir curiosity.

Perhaps someone at the Vatican let it be known the new pope, Leo X, would like to see so small a creature. Perhaps not. At any rate, a preserved hummingbird skin arrived there sometime before 1516 and may have been among the trinkets and treasures sent to the pope in a gift chest from the King of Portugal in 1514.

This may have been the first hummingbird skin to reach Europe, although such a gift could have been sent earlier by Columbus—or any other Spanish mariner—and vanished without record. Columbus did collect many specimens of plants and animals—living and dead—and mentioned doing so in his journals. Few of the live creatures—except the parrots—survived very long and the skins were usually eaten by insects or mice before any artist could make a likeness for the record.

Better fortune was in store for this hummingbird skin and a few other items in the same gift chest—the skin of a larger bird with topknot plumes, a small lizard skin and a stalk of the Indian grain called *maize*. Before they vanished they were seen by the great artist Raphael. And Raphael could not resist bringing them to life with full color.

Raphael was then designing a loggia—a pillared gallery or arcade—for the Vatican. His plan called for Biblical scenes to be painted on the arched spaces crowning each pair of facing pilasters, but he envisioned all sorts of bright-colored flowers and birds and other animals to adorn the pilasters themselves. As he sketched out ideas for his assistant Giovanni da Udine to follow, the exotic new species from the Americas were given a place.

The larger bird with the topknot plume—perhaps a tinamou, quail or plover—was portrayed as a matched pair for the panel on Pilaster Four. For Pilaster Eleven, the choice was a pair of hummingbirds perched among almond branches. The one on the left faces forward, with its long beak cocked upright in a typical, unmistakable hummingbird pose for certain identification. Evidently there had been no accompanying note to explain that these little ones feed on nectar, for the branches offer no flowers for the long beak to probe.

Hummingbird on pilaster in loggia by Raphael, from Volpato, Rome, 1777.

Thus the record is clear, the first pictures of hummingbirds seen by Europeans were done under the auspices of one of the world's most famous artists and were on display in one of the world's most famous buildings by the early date of 1519, when Raphael's work on the Vatican loggia was completed. Few who saw it then knew the design for Pilaster Eleven included a real bird from faraway lands across the Ocean Sea, not just a creature of fable and fantasy, for no detailed description of hummingbirds had yet been written. And even later, when almost every European scholar had read of these smallest birds, few visitors to the Vatican noticed it among the other art or understood its impressive role in hummingbird history.

The first detailed description of hummingbirds in European print would soon follow. This historic account was written by a Spaniard, Gonzalo Fernández de Oviedo y Valdés, who had been a young court page and one of Angleria's pupils when Christopher Columbus first set sail for the Indies. By 1514, Oviedo was experienced enough to be sent to Santo Domingo as a responsible government official. He would continue to serve there for many years, winning royal favor and two governorships.

On one brief voyage home in 1526, he talked so glowingly of Caribbean wildlife and lush vegetation that he was asked to write the official natural history of the Indies. He had already begun collecting material for just such a book, and quickly wrote out a brief account for immediate publication: *De la natural hystoria de las Indias*. Somehow a pirated Italian edition known as the *Sommario* (Summary) was out by December 1534, as printers in Venice, Rome and elsewhere continued to borrow everything about the New World that could slip past Spanish censors.

Meanwhile, Oviedo returned to Santo Domingo, eager to complete his planned history. A large section of this voluminous work was finally published in Spain in 1535 and reprinted in 1547, but the entire work would not be published until 1851. Over the years several reprints of the first book appeared in both Spanish and Italian versions and both were translated to various other languages and widely read. For many Europeans this was their first book on the Americas, the first to tell them of the hummingbird, and they must have read Oviedo's description in awed wonder and delight:

> ... no bigger than the end of a man's thumb ... and of such swiftness in flight that you cannot see the movement of their wings.... The colors shine like those of the little birds artists paint to illuminate the margins of holy books ... and with a bill as delicate as a fine needle. ... The are hardy yet so little I would not dare tell of it if others had not seem them also ...

Oviedo further observed that bird and nest together weighed but twenty-four grains or just two *tomínes*—a unit used by pharmacists and silversmiths in weighing the very smallest amounts. The comparison caught Spanish imagination and hummingbirds were soon dubbed *los tomineos*—a label roughly translated as 'little bits' or 'least ones.'

Oviedo also coined an actual name, a two-word label that would be widely used—*pájaro mosca* (bird fly, meaning a bird of fly size). To emphasize its smallness, he sometimes wrote *pájaro mosquito* (little bird fly), giving *mosca* a diminutive ending.

Small size was all he intended to convey with the *mosca* or *mosquito* tag. But his readers were looking for marvels and happily assumed this was a fantastically weird creature actually half-bird and half-insect. Word soon spread that it began life as an insect and would eventually transform itself into a bird, all in one burst of magic. A few travelers to the Indies even boasted they had witnessed this metamorphosis with their own eyes.

Some stay-at-homes believed the tale, some did not. And to be fair, it must be conceded the tale-spinners might have thought they were telling the truth. Because they could have observed a moth, not a bird. Hawk moths of the family *Sphingidae* are about hummingbird size and come out at twilight to sip nectar from flowers much as hummingbirds do. Like all butterflies and moths, they begin life as caterpillars and then encase themselves in a pupa or coccoon to emerge as winged creatures—a process that seems like magic even to modern eyes.

Also, in further exoneration, a new-hatched hummingbird is such a scrawny little mite, with no more than a few tufts of almost invisible down on its naked body, that it could easily be mistaken for an insect. Seeing it turn into a feathered beauty—even though the change takes a reasonable three weeks instead of magical minutes—seems like fantasy, too.

Spanish writers in the Indies would soon be crediting hummingbirds with even more fantastic powers. One of the first to do so in writing was the scholarly Franciscan friar Bernardino de Sahagún, who came to Mexico in 1529 and stayed until his death some sixty years later. Although his work would not be published for another three centuries, it still deserves its mid-sixteenth century date and full tribute. Sahagún learned enough of the difficult language spoken by the Aztecs of Mexico to write his history in both that Nahuatl tongue and in Spanish, with the two texts printed in parallel columns. He also included illustrations—some grotesque, some delightful—and the three small panels showing hummingbirds among native flowers are some of the most appealing. He also gave descriptions of several different hummingbirds, brief and factual.

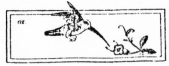

Hummingbirds, from Bernardino de Sahagún, Mexico, ca. 1550.

Along with his factual observations, Sahagún made the astounding statement that hummingbirds could die—indeed, did die each winter—and then return to life by some unknown means. "It rejuvenates itself," he wrote. "It awakens, comes to life." Word of this miracle reached Spain long before Sahagún's book was in print, and there would be travelers to aver they had seen this resurrection take place.

Sahagún went on to record that Spaniards called birds with this power *pájaros resucitados* (revived birds), while the Aztec name was *vitzitzilin* or *vitzili*, still with the same meaning. He did not make it quite clear whether he believed their revival was from true death or merely a deathlike trance. Nor did he say how long they could remain in this state and still return to life—whether for an entire winter (as some moths and butterflies do in the pupa stage) or for some shorter period. He reported it as actual fact, something that had been witnessed, not just recounted as myth or fantasy.

Most Europeans of this era accepted an ability to return from the dead as part of hummingbird mysteries. As the historian Antonio Herrera would summarize it in 1601:

> There are some birds in this country of the size of butterflies, with long beaks and brilliant plumage... Like the bees, they live on flowers and the dew which settles on them. And when the rainy season is over and the dry weather sets in, they fasten themselves to a tree by their beaks and soon die. But in the following season when the rains return, they come to life again.

Meanwhile, Sahagún—and others who cared to ask—learned that Aztec *vitzitzilin* could name any hummingbird but especially the species that most often practiced torpidation. A descriptive word was usually added to the term to distinguish the species. The Aztecs also used another general name—*huitzil* or *huitzitzil*—which translates several ways. The most probable version is 'shining one with a weapon like a cactus thorn,' which reduces to 'shining thornbill.' The hummingbird bill is indeed a weapon, as well as a useful tool for sipping nectar, since angry hummers defending their territory wield it like a war club to drive off unwelcome invaders.

These Nahuatl names first recorded by Sahagún were listed again in the 1570s by the famous court physician Francisco Hernández when he came to Mexico for a five-year study of plants, animals and minerals used by the Aztecs in medical treatment. His finished manuscript—sixteen folio volumes of text with twelve hundred pictures drawn by his son Juan and various Aztec artists—was sent to the king in royal wrappings of blue vellum with gold and silver lacings and buckles. It was stashed away in the royal archives where it burned to ashes in a palace fire in 1671. Luckily, several copies of the text and of some of the illustrations had been kept elsewhere. A Spanish edition was published in Mexico in 1615 referring to the hummingbirds as *avecillas*. This is a more general term for 'little birds' than Oviedo's *pájaros*, which could also mean 'sparrows.' A German translation of Hernández appeared in 1628, Latin texts in 1635 and 1651 (with his name misspelled Fernández) and became standard authorities.

Hernández coined a basic Latin name for hummingbirds, *Aves Varias* (Many-Colored Birds), praised their beauty and noted the throat was often of contrasting hue. He also told how Indian artists used the bright feathers like paint in creating pictures. Since medicine was his field, he did not forget to mention that powdered hummingbird flesh was considered a cure for epilepsy, but did not add—as Sahagún did—that it was also used to treat pustules, even though it was thought to make the patient sterile.

Like Sahagún—and almost every other writer—Hernández explained that a hummingbird depends on flower nectar for survival and without it would fasten itself within a tree trunk crevice by its beak and hang there lifeless until the returning rainy season brought the flowers—and the bird—back to life "as if released from entombment." This was on official record, he added, lest someone think it a jester's hoax. And the editor of his Spanish text made further explanation with: "In lands where flowers are alive all year, so are these birds."

XOÐHOITZITZILIN

Hummingbirds, from Francisco Hernández, Mexico, ca. 1570.

Hernández noted that each kind of hummingbird had an Aztec name of its own. To Europeans, most of these were tongue-twisting combinations of consonants with only a few vowels and therefore difficult to pronounce and all but impossible to spell. (See Chapter 8.) Consequently, most Spaniards ignored the Aztec names and used Oviedo's *pájaro mosca* (fly bird) or *tomineo* (little bit). Anyone wanting an American name for an American species found it far easier to use one from the first tribe Columbus had encountered. These people were the Taino of the Bahamas, whose language was used in Cuba and Haiti and other nearby islands and by mainland Caribs from South America. In Taino, the hummingbird was *colibrí*—as the Spaniards wrote it, matching the liquid sound to their own syllables. Its meaning was set down as 'sky spirit,' 'magic sky bird,' 'god bird' or 'sun god bird.'

Eventually many Europeans would adopt this Taino name. The French, Italians and Portuguese kept the Spanish spelling, but the English matched their own phonics with colibry, colibree or colibrie. The German spelling is *kolibri* now as it was centuries ago, and the Dutch still prefer *kolibrie,* or *kolibrielje,* with an added diminutive.

Meanwhile, imaginative Spaniards began inventing a few picturesque names in their own language—names still in use in lands that were once Spanish colonies. *Picaflor* (flower piercer), *chupaflor* (flower sucker or sipper) *chuparosa* or *chupamyrta* (sucker of roses and myrtle) are the four most often heard today. Another Spanish name is *joyas voladores* (flying jewels). Other Spanish names may be translations of old Indian names, for other tribes besides the Aztecs had their names for hummingbirds.

In Brazil, where Portuguese, not Spanish, is the language, early settlers had first used Oviedo's 'little bit' label, spelling it *tomineo* or *tomenco.* They also coined the name *chupamel* (honey sipper), but the one most often heard today is even fancier—*beija-flor* (flower kisser).

Meanwhile, back in Europe, Oviedo's first brief natural history of 1526 was being translated into other languages and read eagerly. His description of the 'fly bird' was the basis for the first reports of hummingbirds published in Latin, French, and English, and by chance all three accounts appeared in the same year of 1555.

LATIN

Latin became an international language for western Europe when the all-conquering armies of the Caesars gave Rome its far-spread empire. After Rome's final defeat, its former colonies emerged as independent nations, each ready to resume its former language. However, new rulers of those nations soon discovered they still needed Latin for international communication. It was the only common tongue they shared, and so of necessity Latin became the language for diplomacy, trade and every other kind of exchange. Since all available text books were those left by the Romans, Latin also became the language of learning.

The universities saw no reason to change. Professors continued to deliver all their lectures in Latin and assigned lessons in books written in Latin. Students were expected to talk with their teachers—and with each other—as fluently in Latin as in their homeland tongue. This had one great advantage: a scholar could study anywhere in Europe without the need to learn any language other than Latin.

Each student and teacher was required to Latinize his name, re-spell it as necessary and apply the proper ending to conform to the rules of Latin grammar, even though this could mean he would be *Petrus* (instead of Peter) to answer roll call, but *Petri* when he signed his name as author of an assigned theme.

In school or out, a scholar was supposed to use Latin for all important writing, and that meant someone had to devise a Latin name for hummingbirds. Pedro Martir de Angleria, Queen Isabella's court scholar, had been first to refer to them in Latin in a letter written in 1516 (but not published until 1530). Rather than naming the birds, he had just applied a descriptive term designating them as smaller than a kinglet, warbler or wren.

In 1555 an official Latin name would be published in a

new history of birds by Conrad Gesner of Zurich, noted physician, naturalist and scholar. His reputation had been made in 1551 with the first volume of a two-part history of animals that described all the quadrupeds then known. Now this third volume on birds would add to his international fame, and the hummingbird achieved its scholarly Latin label—*passer muscatus* or *muscatus passer*, the former used in his heading, the other in the text. Either way, he was taking his cue from Oviedo's *pájaro mosca*, although *muscatus* means 'fly-like' rather than 'fly.'

Unfortunately, some of his readers mistranslated *muscatus* as 'musky' and those who forgot that *passer* could name any small bird thought he described a musky-scented sparrow. Careful readers, however, would not have been misled, for he explained that *muscatus* implied small size, a bird little larger than a bee, the smallest ever seen.

Conrad Gesner, from Jardine's *The Naturalist's Library*, Edinburgh, 1834.

Gesner had this information—his first and only knowledge of hummingbirds—in 1552 from a Milanese naturalist who gave him Oviedo's description. So Gesner's report on small size, twenty-four-grain weight of bird and nest, shining variable colors, needle-like bill and bold defense of nest are all in Oviedo's phrasing.

Later writers reported that Gesner had seen a dried skin, but he did not say so in his book. Also, he did not publish a picture, as he might have done if a skin had been available for the artist to study. Incidentally, he stated that the bird came from India—the term he used for Columbus' Indies—causing some further confusion for readers.

The hummingbird now had a scholar's Latin label for official use, although no other writer was obligated to use it. Any naturalist in those days could coin any Latin phrase he pleased to label a plant, animal or mineral. Travel books and other light reading could be in current languages, but scholarly rank called for Latin. In fact, scholarship also seemed to call for coining a new label, not copying any already in print.

Gesner's reputation was so impressive, however, that many writers would copy his names, especially for species they themselves had not seen. Many Europeans were likely to accept *passer muscatus* as an official scholarly term, but not the French. Even in 1555 there was a feeling among French writers that their language was as scholarly as Latin and far more patriotic for a Frenchman to use.

FRENCH AND MORE LATIN

Two naturalists, Pierre Belon and André Thevet, first described hummingbirds in French texts. Belon was in print in 1555 with his scholarly study of birds of all kinds, *L'Histoire de la Nature des Oyseaux*. Thevet's travel book of his Brazilian adventures would not be published until two years later. But his trip had begun in 1555 when he first reached Brazil. Before the year was out he had seen hummingbirds and learned a new name for them from the Tupi Indians.

Both Belon and Thevet had previously won acclaim for their skill as writers and naturalists with their travel books on the Middle East. Both had also contributed valuable material to Conrad Gesner for his books on quadrupeds and had their information acknowledged in print. Now Belon dared to rival Gesner's Latin book on birds with his French text. As might be expected, Gesner (and his Latin) got all the scholarly applause. The importance of what Belon had to say was eclipsed by the fact that he was saying it in French. Some critics said openly that he had written in French only because he wasn't scholarly enough to write in Latin.

Pierre Belon.

Belon may well have lost some of his fluency in Latin over the years since he left college classrooms. But so had many other well-educated Frenchmen who were still eager to read books written with a scholar's accuracy. And Belon was still a scholar, as he had always been. He had completed his medical studies in Paris in 1540 and when he let his interest in botany and natural history be known, his sponsors had given him one year of study at the University of Wittenberg and then another in Padua. He then began further travels on his own until some of his influential and wealthy friends back in Paris arranged for him to accompany certain diplomatic envoys to various lands in the Middle East.

Travel suited Belon far better than classroom study. He was eager to learn about nature through observation, not just through reading what others had written. Wherever he went —from Venice to Constantinople, Crete, the Holy Land, or Egypt—he haunted the early morning markets where fowlers and fishermen brought their catch, always hoping to find some unknown species or to get a better look at a familiar one. At every seaport he was down at the docks begging sailors to sell him—or at least show him—any skins of birds or beasts brought back from far places. The enormous curved bill of a toucan from Brazil was one such trophy, and he would put it on display in the new museum he opened when he returned to Paris in 1549—a museum that was soon accounted one of the best in Europe.

Perhaps he had first heard about hummingbirds from some sailor, or at least had a hint that such small birds existed. The first authentic account he could rely on probably came from the Milanese naturalist who had supplied Gesner with Oviedo's description. At least Belon knew both *passer* and *pájaro* had been used as names, for he included in his own book a somewhat disgruntled reference to "men of authority, doctors and savants" who had assigned to themselves the right to classify this unusual bird among the sparrows.

Belon was far more precise than Gesner in grouping birds according to actions, appearance and anatomy as modern classifiers do. Except for broad general groups—such as *Passeres* for all sparrow-like birds—Gesner usually followed the alphabet. Belon was the main writer since Aristotle to achieve scientific grouping. He defined six groups of birds: raptors, waterfowl with webbed toes, waterfowl with separated toes, terrestrial birds (from ostriches to larks), large arboreal birds and small arboreal birds. He was the first to show likenesses between bird and human skeletons. As another first, his birds were pictured in typical habitat or with a typical food. He also gave each bird's name in classic Greek—with a quotation from Aristotle if one was available—and listed the Latin name used by Pliny, the foremost naturalist of first-century Rome. This idea of verifying his French text with names from classic scholars was one of Belon's most important contributions—one for which he seldom gets credit.

Since hummingbirds are strictly New World birds, Belon had no classic names to identify them. But someone gave him two Latin labels. One, Gesner's translation of Oviedo's *pájaro mosca,* he turned into French as *le petit mouchet*—the 'very little fly.' However, he mistook the term's metaphorical use and assumed it indicated a bird with an all-insect diet, a kind of flycatcher.

The second label, *Passer rubi*, was misunderstood also. He thought it came from *rubeta,* Latin for 'thornbush' or 'briars,' and therefore indicated a bird living only among thorny shrubs and brambles. Hummingbirds may feed and nest amid such plants, but not exclusively, and the root was probably *rubeo,* 'to turn red,' or *rubesco,* 'to grow red, to become suffused with color.' Or perhaps it was an abbreviation (often used in old texts) for Italian *rubino,* 'ruby.'

Belon had little information to share with readers, but he used what he had to say that this *mouchet* was different from other flycatchers. What really made it unique among all birds was the size and shape of its bill, which was *delie et longuet*— 'delicately thin and somewhat long.' Nevertheless, because of that *passer* label, he had to assume it was like the two most common sparrows of Europe—the House Sparrow and the European Tree Sparrow. He asked his artist to sketch a sparrow-like bird with a fly in its thin bill and perched amid briars, and thus his *petit mouchet* is pictured. Scant resemblance to any hummer!

For the next century—or even longer—most artists had to work from second-hand descriptions of hummingbirds, or at best from a dried skin. So the picture in Belon's book wasn't too different from some of those that followed it into print. Nor had Belon heard about the murmuring music of vibrating wings, but only that the song of the *mouchet* was 'rather pleasant.' There was much more for André Thevet to learn in actual observation in Brazil.

Thevet lacked Belon's scholarly approach, but he was equally ardent in his desire to study nature for himself. He was so eager to know the strange birds and other wildlife of the Americas that he signed on with a group of French Protestants who had been promised religious freedom in return for founding a colony in Brazil. Portugal had already claimed this area, but had done little to hold it, and the French were desperate enough to risk a take-over. Thevet was certainly odd man out in this Protestant company, for he was a Franciscan friar of the Cordelier Order. However, he had influential friends at court, including Catherine de Medici, and no doubt was given a place in return for an unbiased report of events.

Unfortunately, the little colony on Rio de Janeiro Bay did not last long, for the Portuguese were more protective than the French had supposed. But Thevet's book was a great success. Its title—*Les Singularités de la France Antarctique*—was more than a little misleading by today's geographical terms, for to Thevet Antarctica was anywhere south of Florida, and his travels warranted his assuming the title of cosmographer with full royal approval. According to the English translation published by Thomas Hacket in 1568, there was one little bird he would never forget...

> no bigger than a great fly, which for all it is so tiny is so fair to see that it is impossible to see any that is fairer; the bill is somewhat long and slender, and the color is grayish, and although to my judgment it is the least bird living under the sky, nevertheless it sings very well with a song pleasant to hear.

In spite of song and color, this has to be a hummingbird—perhaps seen only in rainy season with no sun to bring out its full brilliance. Thevet gave its name in Brazil as *gouambuch*, a Tupi Indian word he did not translate and few readers ever repeated. Perhaps it was put aside because Jean de Léry, who had also been in Brazil, published a revision of Thevet's work in 1584 using the spelling *gonambuch*, while Georg Marcgrave, a later German naturalist spelled it *guainumbi*.

Among the few to mull over this spelling riddle was the Flemish scholar Charles de L'Ecluse, who wrote in Latin as Carolus Clusius. In 1605 he gathered everything he could find about this strange, tiny bird from the Americas for his *Exo-*

Hummingbird, from Charles de L'Ecluse, Antwerp, 1605.

Hummingbird, copied from de L'Ecluse in Johnston, Amsterdam, 1657.

ticorum Libri, a collection of European writings on plant and animal oddities recently brought to Europe from foreign lands, especially the West and East Indies. He did not mention what Gesner or Belon had published about the hummingbird, but he quoted Oviedo and several other Spanish texts. Among these was a 1577 account with proof from Cardinal Paleotti that a hummingbird skin had already been displayed in Italy. Although it was tagged 'from Mexico' with the name *çinçoni* (a phonetic match for *zunzon, tsintsin* and other echoic names from Mexico given in various Spanish-Mexican accounts), today's readers may hazard the guess that Paleotti's hummingbird may have been the same specimen seen by Raphael.

Hummingbird, copied from de L'Ecluse in Marcgrave, The Netherlands, 1648.

In addition, L'Ecluse noted in surprise that only Thevet and Léry made any reference to hummingbird song. Thevet had stated only that the song was 'quite pleasant' but Léry claimed it was so continuous and so musical that it even rivaled the voice of the nightingale. Of course he must have heard the murmur of vibrating wings, not a voice, and this humming is certainly continuous and even musical, though no rival for the nightingale song to most listeners.

Léry also noted this bird was so small it could even perch on a stalk of the native Brazilian grain, which he identified as *mayzum*—obviously a Latinized spelling of the Taino Indian word for corn (*mays, maiz*), a plant as all-American as the hummingbirds and considerably sturdier than the European grains L'Ecluse and his readers had in mind.

More important, L'Ecluse described and pictured a hummingbird known in Brazil as *ourissia*, 'sunbeam bird.' Its preserved skin had been on exhibit in the museum of Jacob Plateau of Tournai, Belgium, since 1600, and Plateau had provided a print tinted in the bird's natural colors. He added a description so detailed there is little doubt in identifying the Ruby-topaz Hummingbird, ranging from Brazil to Bolivia and the Guianas:

> ... at one time its feathers appear black, then ashen, later rose-colored, and then blood red and finally its head catches the sun's rays with all colors reflected.... Furthermore, this bird was, as shown in the portrait, three inches long from the tip of its pointed beak, to the end of its tail; its head and beak together making up half this length; the wings extending almost to the tail tip of about equal length; the back barely an inch in between; this and the sides were of dark ashen color, the belly also ashen; the tail feathers dimly reddish and on the extreme tips black; neck and throat feathers beautifully colored with red, gold and yellow, all blending,which the sun touches with shining radiance, changing as it turned its head; beak very thin and pointed, but from the start very black; four toes arranged as in other small birds, three in front, and the fourth behind...

So vivid a presentation should have put the word *ourissia*

in circulation at once, but—like *gouambuch*—it remained an esoteric term for the printed page. However, L'Ecluse did help perpetuate the fiction that hummingbirds are half-fly, half-bird. With his testimony added to Belon's *mouchet* and with the 'fly-bird' label from both Gesner and Oviedo, the common French name for hummingbirds became *oiseau-mouche*. It was heard both in Paris salons and in the faraway French colonies in Canada soon after L'Ecluse's book was off the press in 1605. There, in Quebec in 1634, the Jesuit missionary Paul LeJeune wrote of the *oiseau-mouche* in his official reports, suggesting, however, that 'flower-bird' was a more fitting name than 'fly-bird.' It was, he said, "one of the rarities of the country and a little prodigy of nature. God seems to me more wonderful in this little bird than in the largest animal."

Two decades later—in 1658—another intrepid French traveler, César de Rochefort, returned from America to write his Caribbean memoirs and assured readers of his *L'Histoire des Iles Antilles* that these little birds were known everywhere in that area by the old Taino-Carib name *colibrí*. Like the Spaniards, the French would find this Indian word easy to say and remember. They later used it as a classifying term for certain kinds of hummingbirds, but it did not replace *oiseau-mouche*. Also, French colonists in the Caribbean presently coined a few labels of their own, imitating the bee-like buzz of rustling wings with *frou-frou, murmures, and bourdoneur*.

Farther northward, English colonists already had the same idea of matching the name for this little bird to the sound of its wing music. After all, didn't you often hear the humming before you saw the flashing wings?

ENGLISH, AT HOME AND IN THE AMERICAN COLONIES

Richard Eden of London, gentleman, historian, and scholar, gave English readers their first glimpse of hummingbirds in his book, *Decades of the Newe Worlde or West India*, published in 1555. He borrowed his title from the published letters of Pedro Martir de Angleria, which were planned as a set of ten, and also translated much of de Angleria's text.

Eden's description of the hummingbird, however, came from Oviedo. He repeated the comments of thumblet size, fast-beating wings, colors that glowed like those in the margins of holy books and almost everything else Oviedo had mentioned in awed wonder. But for some reason—perhaps because his logical mind rejected the half-bird, half-fly fantasy—he identified them only as 'very lyttle byrdes.'

A few years later—1568—Thevet's travelogue was translated to English by Thomas Hacket as *The Newfounde Worlde or Antarctike*. Now English readers had a chance to use the Tupi word for hummingbird—and rejected it as the French had done. Oddly, they did accept other Taino and Tupi animal names Thevet recorded. *Tapir, toucan, coati, agouti, manatee, hutia, cavy* and *tattou* (for armadillo) all were introduced to English print in Hacket's translation.

Not until 1604 would the English find an acceptable name for hummingbirds. It appeared in Edward Grimston's translation of a natural history of the Indies by the Jesuit missionary, José de Acosta, who had served in Peru and Mexico. In those lands, Acosta wrote, he had seen birds so small and so flutter-winged that it was difficult to know whether they were birds, bees or butterflies. Like Oviedo, he measured them by *tomínes* and so called them *tominejos*.

Grimston repeated this Spanish word without translation, apparently thinking most readers would understand the 'little bit' implication. Those who wanted a precise definition could have consulted Minsheu's *Spanish Dictionary* of 1599 and learned that a Spanish *tomín* was "near the weight of an English sixpence." Perhaps more than one Englishman flipped a sixpence in his fingers thereafter, marveling at a bird of such lightness. At any rate, Oviedo's comparison came through Acosta's hands to Grimston and thus to English awareness, and since *tomineios* (or some similar spelling) was reasonably easy to remember, it was widely accepted in England as the only name to use in the early 1600s.

Acosta's text was translated again in 1625 in a hodgepodge collection of re-told travel tales by Samuel Purchas giving *tomineios* further status. Even as late as 1693 the term was given a Latinized face lift as *tomineus* for a scholarly British journal. However, English colonists in America had long since come up with their own choice of names for these only-in-America birds.

The first English-born American to make note of the hummingbirds on a printed page was the famous Captain John Smith, one of the founders of Jamestown Colony in Virginia. He was the colony's chief historian, with the first of his several volumes published in London in 1608 and the longest in 1624—a general history of Virginia, New England and Bermuda. Small hummer size was what caught his eye. "Scarce so big as a wren," he marveled, using the same comparison as de Angleria had done with his "less than a kinglet."

The captain added that some were red, some blue—suggesting he was a bit color-blind. Or perhaps he had never seen those emerald-green back feathers in good light. Nor had he asked his Algonkin Indian neighbors, Chief Powhatan and his daughter Pocahontas, what they called these birds, although he recorded many another Algonkin word in his books.

Apparently Smith had not yet heard the humming wing sound, either. Just who first came up with today's echoic name is impossible to trace now. But it was surely coined in some English-American colony where the sound could be heard—not in England where only preserved skins were known. Both *hum bird* and *humming bird* were in New England speech by the 1630s and *hummer* would soon follow.

First on a printed page was *Humbird,* appearing in *New Englands Prospects* by William Wood, published in London in 1634. Wood had come to Massachusetts Colony in 1630 and he went back to England four years later expressly to see this book through the press. Once that was accomplished, he returned to New England and settled down near what is now the city of Lynn, Massachusetts.

The book sold well, and English readers found much to mull and marvel over, especially a bird:

> ...one of the wonders of the Countrey, being no bigger than a Hornet, yet hath all the dimensions of a Bird, as bill and wings with quills, Spider-like Legges, small clawes. For colour shee is glorious as the Rainebowe, as shee flies shee makes a little humming noise like a humble bee; wherefore shee is called Humbird.

And he added that an Indian *sagamore* (chieftain, king) could always be recognized by the humbird skin worn as an ear pendant. No one of low rank was allowed such an ornament. Any reader who had been to the Caribbean would have nodded, remembering that Taino Indians also had such a rule. Indeed, the hummingbirds there were sometimes called *caciques*, the Taino word for king or chieftain.

In 1643, colonist Roger Williams in Rhode Island noted that the Narragansett Indians had the same custom, using their word *sachem* for both their leaders and the little birds used as ear pendants. A century later, Swedish traveler Pehr Kalm reported that throughout New England these smallest birds were called *king birds* for the regal way they put larger birds to flight. Today, kingbird refers to certain flycatchers, but two hundred years ago the hummingbirds may have shared the name. Certainly both are known for putting larger birds to flight.

In 1637 Thomas Morton, another New England colonist, used *hummingbird* in his book *New English Canaan*. "A curious bird," was his summary, "no bigger than a great Beetle." the name spread quickly to other colonies, for in 1657 Richard Ligoner in the Barbados would write "That which we call the humming bird, much less than a Wren, not much bigger than a humble bee...never sitting but purring with her wings all the time she stayes with the flower...."

As word of these tiny rainbow-hued wonders spread over the ensuing decades, English naturalists began dunning American acquaintances with pleas for preserved skins and any descriptive details they could provide. From London, Francis Willughby, who was hard at work on a new method of classification, made his appeal straight to governor John Winthrop of Connecticut. Winthrop complied, sending the only nest he had been able to find, as well as a skin, but his package did not arrive. In October 1670 he tried again—successfully—enclosing this note:

> I send you withal a little Box, with a Curiosity in it, which perhaps will be counted a trifle, yet 'tis rarely to be met with even here. It is the curiously contrived Nest of a Humming Bird, so called from the humming noise it maketh whilst it flies. 'Tis an exceeding little Bird, and only seen in Summer, and mostly in Gardens, flying from flower to flower, sucking Honey out of the flowers as a Bee doth; as it flieth not lighting on the flower, but hovering over it, sucking with its long Bill a sweet substance. There are in the same Nest two of that Birds Eggs. Whether they use to have more at once, I know not. I never saw but one of these Nests before; and that was sent over formerly, with some other Rarities, but the Vessel miscarrying, you received them not.

Francis Willughby, from Jardine's *The Naturalist's Library*, Edinburgh, 1834.

This time the package arrived and Willughby soon knew more about hummingbirds than most European stay-at-homes. Nevertheless, his classification system was so general he could assign it only to the category for small birds with slender bills. He did not keep the governor's letter to himself, however, but published it in London's *Philosophical Transactions*. The editor, obviously entranced, added a footnote explaining that he himself had weighed the eggs and found one to weigh 5 grains and the other 1½. Nest and eggs together came to only twenty-four-grains. For good measure, he informed his readers this bird was known in the Caribbean as *colibry*—a name he'd culled from a 1666 translation of César de Rochefort's *Histoire des Iles Antilles*, evidently the Taino word's first appearance in an English publication.

English readers would hear of the *colibry* again in 1674 in *An Account of Two Voyages* by the inveterate traveler John Josselyn of Scarborough, Maine. Somewhere in his roaming Josselyn had picked up the tale of hummers as 'return-to-life' birds and gave *viemalin* as his version of their Aztec name. He hailed this little one as "the rising or waking Bird, an Emblem of the Resurrection and the wonder of little birds."

Two years earlier in another book, *New-Englands Rarities*, Josselyn preferred *hummingbird* to *colibry* and added a sketch of its favorite wildflower—known to him as Touch-Me-Not Balsam, but more often listed now as Jewelweed or Impatiens. Both as a wild plant and as cultivated varieties, it is still a hummingbird favorite. Josselyn knew his hummers.

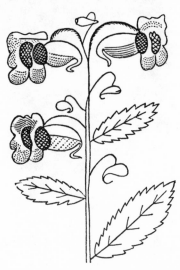

Touch-Me-Not Balsam (Humming Bird Tree), from Josselyn, London, 1672.

He also knew the story that they could "sleep all winter" and offered no denial. "Not to be seen till Spring," he testified, "at which time they breed in little Nests made up like a bottom of soft Silk-like matter, their Eggs no bigger than white Pease."

About this time, colonist John Bannister in Virginia was also trying to ship hummingbird skins back to English enthusiasts, not always with success. At least once all the trouble of drying a female Ruby-throated in its feathers was lost when the cockroaches gobbled it down for a midnight snack. He tried again, this time with the handsomer male, and succeeded. One of his neighbors, a Huguenot refugee named Durand lately come from France, wrote that he'd seen hummingbirds "dressed and dried in the oven to sell later in England for as much as eight pounds sterling each." Obviously, all the traffic in hummingbirds was not just a matter of colonial goodwill.

In 1693 an interview in the *Philosophical Transactions* added further data on the "Hum Bird." Dr. Nehemiah Grew, noted botanist, returned from America with this description:

> The color a shining green, something to resemble our English Drake-heads . . . the weight the tenth part of an ounce Avoirdupoize . . . the nests made of Cotton-Wool, in form and bigness of the Thumb of a Man's Glove. . . . They feed by thrusting their Bill and Tongue into the blossoms of Trees, and suck the sweet Juice of Honey from them; and when he sucks he sits not, but bears up his Body with a hovering Motion of his Wings.

In spite of having seen hummingbirds in America, Grew was guilty of error when he declared the wings were not responsible for the humming sound because they were "too small to strike the air hard enough to make any noise." Other supposed authorities were just as positive that neither the hummers nor any other bird could fly backward. Hummingbirds just "fell backward" out of a flower according to George Campbell, Duke of Argylle, who evidently assumed his position as an authority in English law entitled him to make this decision.

Most writers, however, were content to marvel at hummingbird mysteries without suspicion. In 1794 James Lumden of Glasgow was one who excelled in ingenious comparisons to catch a reader's imagination:

> The Humming-Bird is the least of all birds: the head, together with the feathers, is of the bigness of a mean-sized sweet cherry; the neck is three-quarters of an inch long; the body an inch and a quarter. The body together with the feathers, is scarce equal in bigness to a Spanish Olive. Its colour is wonderfully resplendent: A green (such as is seen on the necks of Peacocks) with a golden flame colour, and yellow, are so strangely mixed, that being exposed to the sun-beams, it shines admirably. It makes its nest in the boughs of trees, of the bigness of an Holland schilling, and lays very white eggs: two for the most part, of an oval figure, not bigger than pease. It is fed and nourished with honey-dew, and the juice of flowers, which it sucks out of them with its bill. It flies very swift, and makes a humming noise, like a Hornet or Bee; hence it took its name in English of Humming-bird.

Hummingbird, from Lumden, Glasgow, 1794.

Throughout the seventeenth and eighteenth centuries Latin was still considered by many to be the only language for scholarly and scientific writing. However, more and more Latin texts were being translated to modern languages, and more and more serious scholars were following the Frenchman Belon's lead and writing in their own language, adding a Latin name of each species for added authority.

One of the most popular eighteenth century English writers to use this double naming—and so give hummingbirds a name in both Latin and English—was Mark Catesby. As a young man he had been a self-taught dabbler in both art and nature study. In 1712 he sailed for America to visit his sister, who was married to a doctor in Virginia. The visit stretched on for several years as Catesby roamed the countryside, idly reveling in the new species of birds and flowers and other wildlife. He collected a few seeds of the most unusual plants for gifts to English friends and was amazed at their enthusiastic reception. Belatedly, he realized he should have been collecting sketches and descriptions for a book.

In 1722 he returned to America, well equipped with brushes, paints, paper and other supplies, ready to set off on a serious four-year nature survey. His route took him through the Carolinas to Florida and on briefly to the Bahamas before he returned to London to prepare for publication beginning in 1732.

The two-volume set, complete with text in both English and French included 220 plates, the hummingbird No. 65. Like the others it was printed in black and white, ready to be tinted to match his original paintings by a relay of hired colorists. No color presses existed then, and colored illustrations were possible only by painstaking handwork on each printed page as it came from the press.

Hummingbird,
from Catesby,
London, 1732.

The process was quite involved. First the artist had to make an ink copy of his original painting—or hire another artist to do so. Then the ink sketch would be turned over to an engraver to reproduce on a copper plate, just as artists in earlier days had done on wooden blocks. The plate or block would then be coated with ink and run through the press like a page of type, and the coloring would be up to the next relay of workers. Of course the original paintings would be there to serve as guide, and often the original artist would be on hand, too—usually trembling at each false brush stroke or taking over himself to repair the damage.

Catesby realized the talent of the engraver was all important for the success of his illustrations, and he made the extra effort to learn engraving himself. He also did much of the color work himself, and his book quickly gained a high reputation for both accuracy and artistic quality.

He pictured a male Ruby-throated Hummingbird in emerald coat and red gorget thrusting its long needle-like bill into the bright blossom of a trumpet vine. But his English caption was simply "The Hummingbird," followed by a Latin label of his own coinage, *Mellivora avis carolinensis,* "honey-eating bird of the Carolinas."

The picture was charming, the pose and added flower lovely to look at and appropriate. The accompanying text was well written and the Latin label apt. But the lack of an added English term to identify the species is a puzzling omission. Surely Catesby realized that *hummingbird* was a group term applicable to many similar species. Even if only one such bird was found in the English seaboard colonies, he had seen others in the Bahamas and read about those seen elsewhere in the tropics, for he commented on descriptions by André Thevet, Jean de Léry, Georg Marcgrave and Francisco Hernández.

But if Catesby didn't realize the need for more definite labels, others in Europe would soon do so. Obviously it was time for someone with a scientific mind to fill this need by devising a system of nomenclature for worldwide use. Belon had taken the first step toward this goal and Catesby and many others had added their thinking. But there was still a long way to go toward an organized system of scientific classification.

5.

SCIENCE FITS
THE HUMMINGBIRD
INTO ITS SYSTEM

THE ENLIGHTENMENT THAT comes with any era of new
thinking does not occur all at once or with only a single
person responsible. Like the sudden flooding of light when
you flick on an electric switch, many factors and many
workers have been involved over a long period of time.

Yet in the science of biological classification—the system of
giving each individual type of plant or animal a name and a
meaningful place in relation to others of the same general
sort—one man and one date are universally accepted as estab-
lishing the modern era. That man is Carl Linnaeus of

Sweden. The date is 1758, the year in which he published the famous tenth edition of his *Systema Naturae*.

Linnaeus had been devoted to nature study since childhood when he followed his father in tag-a-long trail from yard to garden to woodlot, happily repeating the name of each flower, bird or tree his father pointed out. But in those days nature study was a pastime, not a way to make a living, and so—like many others of similar mind—he made a career in medicine, knowing that botany was considered a main branch of medical science.

In due time he became a member of the medical teaching staff at Uppsala University, with the medical garden in his special charge. Botany would always hold his deepest devotion, but he studied all aspects of nature, and not just from books and preserved specimens, but also in the outdoors— something many naturalists of his day did not even attempt.

He often described his first long nature study walking-tour through Lapland as the greatest learning experience of his career. As a teacher he was so insistent on his students' making such field trips—and those who did found them so rewarding—that at his death they paid tribute by pledging to take a memorial nature walk every year on his birthday. Luckily this fell in the spring, May 23 by the new calendar.

Carl Linnaeus, from Jardine's *The Naturalist's Library*, Edinburgh, 1834.

As a teacher he also realized the great need for an improved system of classification for all the natural sciences, and though he began with such a system for botany, he was resolved to make it complete. The text for this *Systema Naturae* was in Latin, of course. His position demanded no less. His surname had always been Latinized with the proper *-us* masculine ending. His father Nils had so written it on entering college to study for the Lutheran ministry. When Nils graduated and was assigned his first pastorate, he kept the Latinized form for the sake of its added dignity and prestige, and continued to use it. So Carl used it also. When he went to college he Latinized Carl to Carolus, as was required—and wrote it Caroli Linnaei for college papers and his published books, showing the right Latin ending for authorship.

After Linnaeus became famous and was knighted by the Swedish king, he was known in society and court circles as Carl von Linné. When invited to lecture in England, he was addressed as Sir Charles Linné. But for most of the rest of the world he has remained Linnaeus.

Biological classification, as Linnaeus knew it, began in the Old Testament (Leviticus, Chapter 11; Deuteronomy, Chapter 14) when Moses, after listening to the voice of God, set down the identifying features of animals that were—or were not—clean and fit for food. These ancient Hebrew laws first aligned animals by basic habitat as creatures of land, water or air. Land animals were further divided into those that did or did not chew cud, those that had divided or undivided hoofs, those that had to creep and crawl or those that had four good legs for leaping. Water animals were in only two categories— with or without scales. Creatures of the air were also of only two kinds—those that were born with wings and those that at some stage were wingless and could only creep and crawl.

European Christians had long accepted these Biblical definitions. They separated the birds from insects fairly well, but left no place for bats except with the birds—a misfit that would trouble Bible-reading naturalists for centuries. Even Belon had included the bat among the birds, but that good Franciscan friar Sahagún had dared to solve the riddle by declaring feathers were the one thing that belonged to birds. Featherless bats were therefore something else, and Linnaeus rescued them out of limbo by dropping the old Biblical term *four-legged* (*quadrupedes* in Latin) and defining a new category—mammals, those that nurse their young on mother's milk.

In classifying birds, Mosaic laws had given no physical description, but had defined groups by well-known members, using such terms as 'raven-like,' 'all of heron kind,' and 'kites of all sorts.' Most classifiers of later years would use this same technique.

After the Hebrew laws, the next classifying system came from the Greek philosopher Aristotle (384-322 B.C.). He would identify a related group by a well known member— 'dovelike,' for instance—but also by similar habitat, food and foot structure. If the Romans hadn't conquered the Mediterranean world about then, some later Greek savant might have developed Aristotle's system still further. But the Romans did conquer—and paid little heed to Greek or Hebrew lore and languages.

In the first century A.D. the Roman naturalist Pliny presented his meager categories, classifying birds only by foot structure—those with sharply hooked toes, with webbed toes, or with blunt toes. He arranged land animals by size, largest to smallest, and many naturalists of the next fifteen centuries —even the famed Conrad Gesner—generally listed plants and animals only in alphabetical order. Gesner's English translator, Edward Topsell, defended this system by noting that any attempt to classify in similar groups always led to heated criticism, but nobody argued with the alphabet. Therefore, *canary* was under 'c,' not listed as a kind of finch, for instance, and *cat* was not with *lion* or *tiger*. Before Belon's careful work, one of the few attempts at bird classification came from the Emperor Frederick II of Hohenstaufen, an ardent falconer. Besides ranking all hawks, falcons, eagles and other hunting birds according to their skill, he offered numerous comments on birds of all kinds, including observations on migration.

All in all, Linnaeus and other eighteenth century naturalists who felt the challenge of classification had scant foundation for their new systems. Most of them agreed on using the Latin phrase for Nature's World and dividing that realm into three kingdoms—one kingdom each for animals, plants and minerals. Each kingdom was further divided into stairstep groups of closer likeness with various Latin labels. Today we translate most such terms to English, but *genus* and *species* keep the Latin form. Also retained is *genera,* Latin plural of *genus,* and *species* is the same, singular or plural.

In general usage all these terms had much the same meaning as *kind* or *sort.* But for a scientific system, each needed a precise definition to mark a definite step in broader or closer kinship. Linnaeus chose the Latin for 'class' to label his first broad category within a kingdom, followed by order and genus. Each member of a genus he called a species, an individual kind. If some widespread species differed slightly in size or color tones in certain areas, such individuals could be labeled a variant, but species was his basic individual term.

Other writers made different choices. Consequently, one man's order might be another man's genus or class. Also, Greek and Latin names for the individual kinds of birds were so vaguely defined that one man's sparrow could even be another man's ostrich.

Before Linnaeus, species labels were usually four or five Latin words at least. Catesby used six for the Mockingbird, eight for the Heath Hen and thirteen for the tupelo tree. Beginners and experts alike had to learn a bewildering array of lengthy Latin terms. And each time teacher or pupil changed school or text book or went to a different museum to study, there was a whole new set of these tongue twisters to memorize. What confusion!

Linnaeus had been as guilty as the others in using wordy labels and ignoring the names published by earlier writers. But for the tenth edition of his *Systema Naturae in* 1758 he resolved on drastic reform. First, he revised all his earlier labels, limiting each to only two words—a binomial made up of one word to name the genus (the basic group to which a species belongs) and a second word to describe the species. Next he asked every other writer to follow his lead, to revise all their old labels by accepting his binomials. Uniformity, he told them, was essential. Uniformity, brevity and clarity. Every species of plant or animal ought to be listed by the same Latin binomial in every book in every land—regardless of what local names might be. Only a universal binomial system would end confusion.

Many naturalists agreed at once, and adopted all Linnaeus's binomials without protest. But others stubbornly refused. Even if they admitted that the two-word limit was a great idea, they wanted to coin their own binomials. Let Linnaeus give up his and accept theirs! Of course that wouldn't work. Only one person could author the basic list. But the protests went on, and universal acceptance was delayed, and delayed again, for over a century. Zoologists finally met to discuss the matter in an international assembly in Moscow in 1889, but did not reach any agreement until a second meeting in Paris in 1892, with further discussions to follow. Botanists voted acceptance about the same time, and so the twentieth century could begin with at least basic international accord.

Linnaeus's binomials of 1758 were henceforth to be used in all official publications, with his name added in tribute. Any species not on his list would be credited to whoever was first to report it with a binomial and proper description in public print, and his surname would then be added. If more than one classifier claimed credit, the dispute would be settled by the date of the public print. If Linnaeus or anyone else had assigned a species to the wrong genus, a new binomial with the proper genus would supplant the original listing with the original classifier's name enclosed in parentheses.

These agreements led to the need for some organization in each field, in each country, to take responsibility for the official list of species. For North American birds, that organization is the American Ornithologists' Union, and it has published its *Check-list* since 1886, with its sixth and latest revision in 1983.

Meanwhile, there were still older books in print—and some newer ones written—without the Linnaean binomials. Anyone who consults them may find three or four different Latin labels instead of only one, since editors weren't always sure just which usage would please—or offend—potential purchasers and tried to settle the matter by using every label in print. In 1834, for instance, Sir William Jardine of Edinburgh published a many-volumed *Naturalists' Library,* and in listing labels for the Rufous Hummingbird quoted five different authors. Thanks to Linnaeus, today's books need only one label for identification of the Rufous, *Selasphorus rufus.* This specific term was published by the German naturalist Johann Gmelin. As it happened, Linnaeus died on January 10, 1778, just four months before this species was discovered and so never knew of it.

Rufous Hummingbird, by Lizars in Jardine, Edinburgh, 1834.

However, Linnaeus had named sixteen other hummingbirds in his 1758 edition. Actually he thought he had named eighteen, but one proved to be a bird from Ethiopia and the other was the female of a species already identified. He had not seen any of them as live birds, for he had never traveled to the Americas. Apparently he saw only six as preserved skins —one from Albert Seba's museum in Amsterdam and the others from a museum operated by Adolph Friderici in Kassel, Germany. The rest he included on the basis of descriptions published by the British ornithologist George Edwards in his four-volume *History of Birds,* plus confirming descriptions from other reliable naturalists such as Francis Willughby, Charles de L'Ecluse, Mark Catesby, Sir Hans Sloane, Eleazar Albin and Patrick Browne of Jamaica.

In his twelfth edition of 1766 Linnaeus would add four more hummingbirds as described by Edwards and the French naturalist Matthurin Brisson, bringing his classifications of hummingbirds to twenty. All of them were from the tropics except the Ruby-throated, which was the only species for which he listed both sexes.

Linnaeus had asked naturalists to use all his classifying terms, not just the binomials. In naming the class for birds (class is the first subdivision in each kingdom) he chose *Aves,* Latin for 'birds,' and it is now retained in American and English use without translation. According to that wise scholar of the seventh century, Isidore of Seville, *aves* originally meant 'pathless ones' (*a* = no, *via* = path, road) to mark the mysterious way in which birds find their route across uncharted skies. However, the term may also stem from words for omen and prophecy—or the other way around. At least the Romans used birds in various ways to help them read the future.

After assigning hummingbirds to Class Aves, the next step was to place them in an order. Linnaeus had only six such divisions: *Accipitres* for raptors, *Picae* for birds using their beaks to pierce and stab, *Anseres* for web-footed water birds, *Scolopaces* for marsh or water birds with separated toes, *Gallinae* for chicken-like ground-scratchers, *Passeres* for all small birds. At first Linnaeus had placed hummingbirds in this last catchall order, but in 1758 he re-assigned them to the *Picae* with woodpeckers, toucans and parrots.

Within the order, Linnaeus assigned each species to a genus with other species it most closely resembles. He gave hummingbirds a genus all to themselves, as they clearly deserve. To name it he chose the Greek word *trochilos*, first used by that yarn-spinning traveler Herodotus and later repeated by Aristotle, changing it to the Latin -*us* ending instead of the Greek -*os*. This *trochilos,* so Herodotus claimed, was a slender and very agile bird of the Nile that had somehow acquired a reputation for being able to slip in and out of a crocodile's mouth so quickly it could make a meal on the food clinging to the monster's teeth before the crocodile could make a meal of the bird.

Of course, hummingbirds have no bond with either crocodiles or the Nile. But they are small. And Aristotle—or some careless copyist—had also used *trochilos* to name that other very small bird, the kinglet. To Europeans, then, *trochilos* had come to be a name for the smallest birds of all. Since the hummingbirds now filled that category, Linnaeus thought it only logical to make the Latinized *Trochilus* their generic label, the first word of every hummingbird binomial.

Each species needed a unique second word also, and Linnaeus intended to label the Ruby-throated *Trochilus colibri*, using the old Taino word. But somehow, by a slip of his own pen or the carelessness of a copyist or typesetter, the printed word was *colubris*—Latin for snake! This unfortunate error has never been corrected, for Linnaeus believed the accuracy of a binomial wasn't important so long as it was unique and clearly established. He also entered two other specific names —*ourissia* and *tomineo*—which have since been dropped because they were not established as new species. Among his specific names of 1758 still in use are *pella, mosquitus, holosericeus, mellisuga, mellivorus, mango, niger, ruber, cristatus, minimus* and *polytmus*.

Linnaeus now had to find a new genus for the Goldcrest Kinglet, Wren and the Willow Warbler that had so long shared their 'least of all' status. He placed them all in the genus *Motocilla* (little tail waggers) from which they have all been removed by later classifiers. However, each retains the specific names Linnaeus chose.

The hummingbirds, too, have been re-classified in various genera, with only one of the Linnaean twenty—*Trochilus polytmus*, the Streamertail of Jamaica—still keeping its original label. When the new subdivision of family was generally accepted for international use in mid-nineteenth century, the hummingbird family label was Trochilidae, based on the Linnaean generic term. All family names now follow this pattern of adding '-idae' to the basic generic term. The standard ending '-iformes' for names of orders in Class Aves was not adopted by the AOU until 1931. Generic and specific labels are still not uniform, but endings in a binomial agree in gender.

Each order, family and genus is defined by certain features of anatomy, actions and appearance not shared by other groups. Any part of the anatomy, internal or external, may be involved, but foot and beak structure are most often diagnostic factors. For instance, swimming birds with lobed toes are in one order; swimmers with webbed toes in another. Most song and garden birds have separated toes (three pointed forward, one to the rear) and similar wing structure, and are in the same order. Hummingbirds have similar feet, but must be in a different order because of their unique wing structure and variant formation of beak and tongue. They are further separated into genera according to overall size and coloring, throat color, the length, shape and color of wings, tail and beak (whether the base of the beak as it adjoins the forehead is bare or covered with feather tips, whether beak edges are serrate or non-serrate, whether the beak center is ridged or rounded, and whether the tips are straight or de-curved) and whether sexes are alike or different. Usually these generic differences can be precisely determined only in the laboratory with preserved specimens in hand, except for the color clues and the shape of beaks and tails. Twentieth-century AOU classifiers first assigned hummingbirds to an order named *Macrochires* (long-handed) because the forepart of their wing is unusually long. This order was shared by the nightjars and swifts who have rather similar wing structure. In 1931 the

AOU put only swifts and hummingbirds in the order *Micro-podiformes*, meaning 'small-footed,' with each listed in a separate sub-order. Oddly, the name was changed in 1957 to *Apodiformes*, 'footless,' by the AOU *Check-list*. That label still stands, although neither swifts nor hummingbirds are footless.

Several recent classifiers have urged that *Micropodiformes* be restored for the sake of accuracy, but so far the required international approval has not been granted. Nor has there yet been approval for the suggestion that swifts and hummingbirds are too different to share the same order and ought to be separated.

Linnaeus himself would probably have given humming-birds more distinctive classification if he had been able to study live birds in their native land. He certainly wished he had been able to do so, and he often asked friends and former pupils traveling abroad to send him live specimens of every kind for study. They did so whenever possible. But transporting live hummingbirds seldom succeeded. Few people realized the birds feed on insects and pollen as well as nectar and need this protein to survive. Captives were given only sugar water or honey water and they usually died before the long sea voyage across the Atlantic was completed.

One fortunate Englishwoman reported that her little cageling survived the ocean crossing and lived a good two months thereafter—undoubtedly because she had provided fresh flowers as well as sugar water. In the 1850s the noted British ornithologist John Gould attempted to prolong life by adding egg yolk to the sugar water. But only one of his several captives was still alive when he reached London—and that lone survivor died two days later. Even as late as 1905, when ocean crossings were somewhat faster, hummingbirds intended for the London zoo lived only a scant two weeks. Therefore, Europeans continued to be denied a glimpse of these fascinating rarities who remained creatures of mystery and a challenge to every naturalist.

In France in 1760 Matthurin Brisson would publish the first serious study devoted entirely to hummingbirds. He acquired descriptions or skins of thirty-six individuals which he first divided into two groups. The smaller species with a straight bill he labeled *mellisuga*, Latin for 'honey-sucker.' Larger ones with curved bills had the label *polytmus*, Latinized Greek for 'many-formed, varied.'

After this small concession to Latin terminology, Brisson followed the trend started by Belon two centuries earlier and used only French for his descriptions and individual names. His name for the Ruby-throated Hummingbird was *L'oiseau-mouche à gorge rouge de la Caroline*—which made a small bow of acknowledgment to Catesby but not even the flick of an eye for Linnaeus's request for uniformity.

This revolt against Linnaean Latin would be continued by the most famous French naturalist of the eighteenth century, Georges Louis LeClerc, comte de Buffon, and Buffon would remain Linnaeus's arch rival. Buffon did accept Brisson's idea of two groups, but even those two Latin labels were lopped off in Buffon's accounting. No Latin allowed, was

Georges Louis LeClarc, comte de Buffon, from Jardine's *The Naturalist's Library*, Edinburgh, 1834.

Buffon's creed. He wrote his encyclopedic studies of nature entirely in French and their popularity proved he had judged his public correctly. However, he did borrow a few American Indian words. His group label for the smaller hummingbirds was *colibrí*, but he called the larger group by the familiar *oiseau-mouche.* To him, the specific name for the Ruby-throated was simply *Le Rubis* (The Ruby). Perhaps he chose it because of the Latin phrase, *Passer Rubi,* Belon had reported, but he didn't say so. He was simply following his rule of using one French word everybody would know instead of two Latin words many readers would neither recognize nor remember. The fact that in some lands Latin was better known than French was a point he didn't consider.

Most Europeans of the time were more concerned with hummingbird beauty and the many uses for their shining feathers than with scientific names. Milliners, dress designers, craftsmen of many kinds all wanted hummingbird feathers for their work. Thousands of the little dried bodies were shipped to Paris and London from Brazil and other tropic ports with no record of how many species might have been wiped out in the slaughter. And the destruction went on at a mad pace for over a century. In London on March 21, 1888, more than twelve thousand skins were sold at a single auction and several thousand more a few weeks later.

Both amateur and serious naturalists vied for these little trophies and displayed them in glass cases as if they were jewels. Rivalry over the display of new species was great, and at least one collector was tempted to win applause with an ingenious fake concocted from feathers of several known species. His work was so skillful that even the established naturalist John Latham verified it as authentic and it was actually accepted for display by the British Museum. Jardine also included it in his *Naturalist's Library,* but mentioned the doubts of authenticity. The doubts must have been proved, for the Harlequin Hummingbird, *Trochilus multicolor,* is no longer on official records.

French and English artists, meanwhile, had their own rivalry underway for the best way to capture the likeness of iridescent hummingbird colors in mere paint. In 1801 Jean Baptiste Audubert claimed the honor of being first to add a dusting of real gold to his palette colors. Most appropriately, the book for which these illustrations were made was entitled *Oiseaux Dorés,* 'Golden Birds.' The text was by Louis Jean Pierre Vieillot, well known for his ornithological studies.

Vieillot also spent some time in the Caribbean and in the United States, and was one author who didn't have to rely on stuffed skins.

In the winter of 1826-27 the French naval vessel *Héros*, under command of Captain August Duhaut-Cilly, was on exploration cruise along the California coast. Aboard in the dual role of physician and naturalist was Dr. Paul Emile Botta, eager to collect new specimens. When the ship anchored at Yerba Buena (San Francisco) he found Padre Tomás at the Spanish mission equally eager to show him a remarkable hummingbird—one that stayed all year instead of migrating southward as all the others did. Botta carefully preserved a skin, and the captain—equally entranced—made admiring entry in his log for January 26, 1827:

> It has head and throat of glowing fire.... When the bewitching little creature alights upon a bare branch, for some short seconds, one would say it was a ruby spheroid, or rather a little ball of red-hot iron giving off a shower of sparks. When several are seen together on the same branch, anyone versed in the marvels of Araby might imagine it a wand set with precious gems....

Back in Paris, Botta would turn over the skin for classification to the current authority on hummingbirds, René Primevère Lesson. Like Buffon, Lesson wrote in French, but he did use a two-word Greek label, coining the generic name *Ornismya* (bird-fly) to replace *Trochilus*. His label for Botta's prize was *Ornismya Anna*, honoring a charming Parisian beauty, Anne de Belle Massena, duchesse de Rivoli. She and her husband, the duke, had sponsored various ornithological collectors abroad and had a magnificent array of hummingbird skins to display in their home. The duke already had his namesake, Rivoli's Hummingbird, which would eventually be changed to the Magnificent Hummingbird in 1983. Luckily the duke did not live long enough to know of his loss.

As it happened, an English naval vessel, HMS *Blossom,* stopped at this same California mission that winter and Captain Frederick W. Beechey also saw the red-hooded hummer that stayed all year. Beechey's log entry had none of the French captain's exuberance, but he did mention the 'rich harvest' awaiting the first naturalist to catalog the birds of this unexplored coast.

Why the *Blossom*'s physician-naturalist, William Collie, wasn't involved is a mystery. He brought back other specimens from the voyage, but apparently not the unknown hummer. At least Lesson was granted first appearance in public print. But someone must have returned to London at this time with a red-capped hummingbird, for George Loddige—botanist and avid hummer collector—had a stuffed male which he allowed Audubon to use as model for portrait #425 in his famous folio. The model for Audubon's female and nest had been sent to him from California by his friend and fellow-naturalist Thomas Nuttall. Meanwhile, Jardine would also use Loddige's bird as the model for an entry in his *Naturalist's Library.*

Many other hummingbird skins were turning up in London in these years for museum display. In 1824 British naturalist William Bullock had gone to Mexico for a six-month tour and became so entranced with these jewel-wings that he brought back several for his nature museum. These sold so quickly that he continued to import others. In 1827 artist-naturalist William Swainson was first to see five new species there and pictured and described all five for a single issue of the *Philosophical Magazine.* As it happens, all five are now also seen in the United States.

The most famous British trochilidist, however, was John Gould whose monograph on this fascinating family would be published in sections from 1849 to 1861, with supplements in 1880-85. He would also contribute superb watercolors for illustrations now prized by art collectors as well as naturalists.

In America, naturalist William Bartram of Philadelphia, who had begun sketching and studying birds at age fourteen in 1753, included the Ruby-throated among the 251 species on his remarkable life list. English collectors gladly paid him

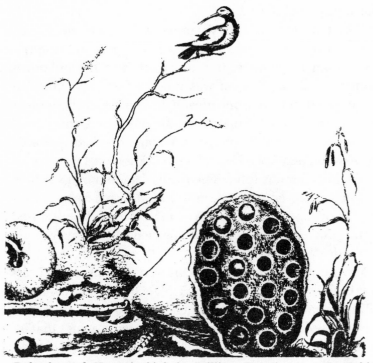

Ruby-throated Hummingbird, by William Bartram, ca. 1767, British Museum of Natural History.

for both sketches and specimens, especially of hummingbirds. One whimsical portrait of a Ruby-throated, is now in the British Museum. But Bartram's greatest contribution to ornithology came through his encouragement of a younger, Scottish-born neighbor, Alexander Wilson, to persevere in fulfilling his dream of painting and describing American birds for book publication.

Wilson did realize that dream. The first volume of his *American Ornithology* came out in 1811 and his portraits of the Ruby-throated Hummingbirds were among his best. Oddly, his title was only "Hummingbird." But his text is presented in a detailed and straightforward manner that rivals any twentieth century account. In reply to the English writers who had been arguing about hummer menu, insisting the long bills were unfit for insect catching, Wilson reported he had watched them catching insects in mid-air for a half-hour at a time "with a dexterity that sets all our other Flycatchers at defiance." As for the old tale about their winter 'sleep,' he had twice held a seemingly dead hummer in his hand and twice had seen mere body warmth or sunshine restore it to lively action.

Alexander Wilson, from Jardine's *The Naturalist's Library*, Edinburgh, 1834.

Wilson's comment on hummingbird torpor is one of the few to be found in nineteenth century books. Most writers rejected the return-to-life story as fable without looking for any trace of truth. And most of them avoided comment on Wilson's testimony as if they were in gentleman's agreement not to notice a fellow writer's slip from fact to fantasy.

Wilson lived to see seven volumes of his work published, and the remaining two volumes he had outlined were completed by his friend George Ord after Wilson's death in 1813.

But no other hummingbird species were added, and that seems odd because the Rufous had been reported by Captain Cook in 1778, with published classification ten years later and subsequent listing in other European books. However, such books weren't always available in Philadelphia then. Or perhaps Wilson might have been influenced by his friends Meriwether Lewis and William Clark who had returned to Philadelphia in 1806 after a two-year trek to the Oregon coast. They had seen hummingbirds—evidently all females— and reported they were the same as those seen back East.

Ruby-throated Hummingbird, by Alexander Wilson, Philadelphia, ca. 1871.

They were wrong, of course. The Ruby-throated Hummingbird of the East has never been seen in Oregon. But females of many hummingbird species are so much alike that no one can be blamed for this misjudgment.

John James Audubon began publishing his famous folios in 1827, and he included four hummingbird species: the Ruby-throated, Rufous, Anna's (which he first named Columbian Hummingbird) and Mango. His paintings continue to receive worldwide acclaim, but modern readers are sometimes put off by the flowery style of his descriptions. An ornate style, of course, was typical of most writers of that era and few of his contemporaries flinched at reading of the Ruby-throated as a:

> lovely little creature moving on humming winglets through the air, as if suspended by magic... glittering fragments of the rainbow... advancing on fairy wings ... with a delightful murmuring sound well-adapted to lulling insects to repose....

The Rufous was given equally flamboyant treatment, but this description was borrowed from his friend and fellow-naturalist Thomas Nuttall who had sent him the specimens from Oregon. This westerner was, so Nuttall and Audubon agreed, a "breathing gem... a magic carbuncle of glowing fire, stretching out its gorgeous ruff as if to emulate the sun itself in splendor... an angry coal of brilliant fire." (Readers of his day probably did not need to be reminded that a carbuncle was a 'ruby' long before it named a 'red and angry pimple.')

Audubon could be factual, too. He described his method of catching birds for study, using an insect net or shooting them with "remarkably small shot or sand" in order not to damage the plumage. He also gave careful details on how far north the Ruby-throateds went into Canada to nest and described some of their favorite flowers—including the same wild Touch-Me-Not-Balsam that John Josselyn had pictured more than a century earlier. Audubon's text, though florid, is usually accurate, because he knew birds thoroughly from hours of patient study. However, he was wrong in stating that male Ruby-throateds stay to help the females with nest building, incubation and nestling care. Perhaps he had been misled by Buffon on this point, for Buffon was also in error. And perhaps Buffon's declaration that the return-to-life story was "a fiction rejected by all intelligent naturalists" also misled Audubon into omitting discussion on this matter.

Audubon's portrait of Anna's Hummingbird, New York, 1840-44.

The popularity of Audubon's work gave all ornithologists added status—as well as added challenge and incentive. Among those to respond was a Mexican naturalist of considerable artistic talent, Rafael Montes de Oca. From 1874 to 1898 his descriptions of hummingbirds were published in *La Naturaleza*, the magazine of the Mexican Natural History Society. In 1875, these essays were issued in a single volume, without his delightful watercolor illustrations of each hummer posed with a native orchid. Color was too expensive, the editor said, and so did every other editor the artist contacted. Before his death, Montes de Oca entrusted these portraits to a friend who put them away so carefully they were not found again until 1963 when they were finally published in a special limited edition. Half the volumes were printed with Spanish text, the other half in English as *Hummingbirds and Orchids of Mexico*. The original paintings are among the treasures in the *Galleria de Arte Mexicana* in Mexico City.

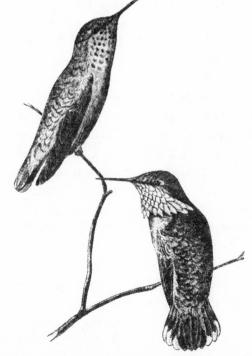

Bumblebee Hummingbird, collected by Rafael Montes de Oca for Ridgway, 1890.

Throughout the nineteenth century, hummingbirds were described with much the same effusive comparisons to jewels, fire-glow flame and fairy magic that earlier chroniclers had used, but there was also renewed interest in the precise terms needed for Linnaean scientific classification. In 1874 Daniel Elliott prepared an excellent monograph on the Trochilidae for the National Museum of the Smithsonian Institution. The next decade brought further knowledge and in 1890 another Smithsonian worker, Robert Ridgway, prepared a special study of hummingbirds for the museum's annual report. It was so well done it was reprinted as a separate volume in 1898, entitled simply *The Hummingbirds*.

Ridgway's illustrations were only ink sketches or black-and-white photographs of paintings (one of them by Montes de Oca who had also provided the museum with its only skin of this species). Ridgeway's book doesn't rival modern texts on illustrations, but his descriptions have a straight-forward approach and thorough analysis that still make them valuable today. However, his research into hummingbird history is much less complete than that possible today, probably because libraries in his day did not have the facilities for inter-library and international exchange now available through microfilm and other media.

With the twentieth century and universal acceptance of Linnaean terminology, earlier books were instantly out of date and in need of revision. This need for revision has continued as a result of the increase in knowledge of avian anatomy that led to frequent changes in assignment to genus and family. New ways of comparing physical likenesses have been developed also, including chemical analysis, and hummingbirds are now listed in well over a hundred genera instead of just the one Linnaeus thought sufficient. Consequently, naming all these genera has been a problem, for each label has to be unique, and classifiers have really stretched their imaginations. Sometimes they have gone far astray from traditional Latin forms and modern researchers are often puzzled over the actual meaning intended.

Variety for common names has been sought also, and there are now fifty-three other English words besides *hummingbird* for Trochilidae names. Nearly half of them describe shape, color or texture of some distinguishing feature—such as lancebill, barbthroat, sabrewing, sicklebill, helmetcrest, awlbill, plovercrest, goldentail, goldenthroat, puffleg, metaltail, thorntail, thornbill, streamertail, firecrown, violet-ear, velvetbreast, jewelfront, plumeleteer. Jewels are frequently found in the names also—emeralds, rubies, sapphires and topazes. And there are fanciful names seldom chosen for other families—woodstar, hillstar, starthroat, mountain-gem, sungem, sunangel, comet, woodnymph, sylph, fairy, even Purple-crowned Fairy and Adorable Coquette!

Lophornis helenae and *Lophornis adorabilis*, from Ridgway, 1890.

In recent revisions, the Adorable Coquette has been more sedately enrolled as White-crested Coquette, but the Latin specific label is still *adorabilis* for convincing proof that even scientists cannot be strictly prosaic when it comes to hummingbirds. Other Latin labels such as *amabilis, bella, fulgens, mirabilis, nobilis,* and *pulcher* (lovable, beautiful, resplendent, marvelous, noble and charming) add further witness. Small wonder, then, that ancient Indian storytellers wove so much magic and mystery into their legends—magic and mystery that still cast their spell as modern naturalists study the ways of the hummingbirds.

6.

WHERE AND HOW TO WATCH HUMMINGBIRDS

HUMMINGBIRD HOT SPOTS

Where do you go to see hummingbirds? Over four hundred years ago Oviedo and Sahagún and Hernández all gave the answer: go where the flowers bloom. And the same advice stands today.

If you want to see as many species as possible in a reasonable length of time—recognizing one briefly and then going on to identify another—you should go where hummingbirds are most numerous and most varied. That means you will head for Ecuador, Colombia, Peru, Venezuela or Brazil. However, unless you know those lands well—and the languages—you will need a guide. Usually you will get best results by joining a nature tour sponsored by a reliable company, museum or similar organization. Such outfits advertise in nature magazines and birdwatching periodicals, and are known to travel bureaus. Join your local natural history museum; they are a wonderful source of information, too.

If you don't want a foreign language conflict, try a tour to any of the Caribbean islands where English is spoken. You'll find many exciting species you can't see at home at the Freeport Botanical Gardens on Gran Bahama Island, for instance, or at the Asa Wright Nature Centre on Trinidad, or other places your travel agent may recommend.

Birdwatchers from eastern Canada who want to see the western species in their own country should try the southeastern corner of British Columbia and go on to the coast. All four western Canada hummingbirds—the Rufous, Calliope, Anna's and Black-chinned—can be seen there in summer. Frequently the Anna's is seen in winter, too.

In the United States, the most hummingbird species on any one safari can probably be seen in southeastern Arizona. Anywhere from Tucson to Nogales and eastward to Portal, Douglas, Green Valley, and Madera Canyon will cover the most likely area. Almost any flower-filled slope in the Chiricahua or Huachuca Mountains should yield a few good sightings. If you haven't contacted a guide and are on your own, look for a well-watered canyon with gently sloping hillsides where flowers can have both sun and shade. Look also for bush clumps and briar patches that provide nesting sites and night roosts, shelter from predators or bad weather. Some of the most successful places are along Cave Creek. Ramsay Canyon, Sycamore Canyon, and Garden Canyon are also mentioned frequently by satisfied hummer hunters. Public camping grounds, motels and resorts are available in the area, and those in charge are used to questions about hummingbirds.

In California, try the Rancho Santa Ana Botanical

Gardens at Claremont, or the South Coast Botanical Gardens at Palos Verdes as well as any other flower-filled spot you happen to find. You can also see captive species at the San Diego Zoo and so familiarize yourself with species you may later see in the wild.

During spring and fall migration, almost any western state could provide a surprise glimpse of new species for the hummer hunter's list. Migrants stop to feed all along the way, wherever flowers bloom or where thoughtful house-holders have syrup feeders ready. In 1981, according to verified acounts in *American Birds,* eighteen backyards in one area of Beulah, Colorado, were prepared for hungry migrants. They welcomed 403 individuals of four different species: Black-chinned, Rufous, Magnificent (Rivoli's) and Broad-tailed. Springdale, Utah, is another favorite migrant stopover.

In Big Bend National Park, Texas, on the Mexican border, eight species of hummingbirds have been seen on the same August afternoon. North Padre Island, Texas, is a good place to watch spring migrants. Far to northward at Crow's Nest Pass, British Columbia, Rufous and Calliope Humming-birds have been seen the same day at the same feeder. One day in 1983, according to the always-helpful *American Birds,* a roving Ruby-throated joined them for one of the farthest westward sightings of this easterner. Another was seen in Truckee, California, in 1984 and others may turn up almost anywhere. In the East, their regular range, good watching places include Powder Mill Nature Reserve in Pennsylvania, Hilltop Arboretum in East Baton Rouge, Louisiana, and Point Pelee National Park in Ontario, Canada. Wintering Ruby-throateds are sometimes seen in Florida Everglades and elsewhere in Dade County and in the Florida Keys.

ATTRACTING HUMMINGBIRDS

If your backyard hasn't attracted hummingbirds so far, a lit-tle extra effort may be all that's needed to make them feel welcome. Check with the nearest nursery or garden shop or Audubon Society for a list of the nectar-rich flowers that do well in your area. And while you're waiting for them to bloom, hang out a syrup feeder.

Be sure to get your feeder out early enough to catch the first migrants, since most hummingbirds looking for nesting sites or rest stops tend to stay where they first find sufficient food—and to return in following years. On the Oregon coast, the first migrants are around in February. Further inland, around Portland, they are usually on hand in March. Those that nest in Wyoming don't usually arrive until late June. Back on the eastern seaboard, Ruby-throated Hummingbirds arrive in mid-April or early May. If you haven't been keeping a calendar for hummingbird arrivals, someone at the nearest Audubon Society surely can provide the dates.

Hang the syrup feeder or potted flowers near your best watching window, even right under the eaves where they will be protected from the weather. The hummers will soon be accustomed to your presence as you look out, and will sip away practically at arm's length. Feeders of various designs and sizes are available at most garden shops. Even variety stores and supermarkets carry them. You can make your own

Identified as *Coeligena iris*, by John Gould, London, 1861.

by punching a hole in the cap of a plastic pill bottle to accommodate a searching hummer bill. Then wind a twist of garden wire around the middle to provide a loop for fastening the bottle to a handy branch or wall hook or the rim of a hanging flower basket.

Just how sweet to make the syrup, without making it too sweet for hummer digestion, has been a matter of much discussion in recent years. Remember, hummingbirds demand more energy — and therefore more carbohydrates — than humans. Hainsworth of Syracuse University conducted tests of the natural sugar content of over forty flowering plants that hummingbirds visit. His tests showed that the natural sugar content of the top twenty-eight favorites matches a ratio of about three or four parts water to one part plain white cane sugar.

Chemically, cane sugar in solution is close to the glucose-fructose-sucrose make-up of nectar, so there is no danger of giving the birds a food their systems can't handle. Honey-water has a similar make-up, but is dangerous, for the honey seldom completely dissolves in water. Even a minuscule glob of honey on a hummer tongue can cling and ferment, and in time cause the tongue to swell so much the bird can no longer swallow and soon dies.

Like most wild creatures, hummingbirds tend to take the food that is easiest to obtain. But they will seldom use feeders exclusively if flowers are available. Also, they will continue their instinctive hunt for insects and pollen, no matter how handy the feeder or how constant its supply. If you have not had hummingbirds in your yard and are putting out a feeder for the first time, start with one of the smaller sizes and make sure it has a red cap and a red circlet around the nozzle-tip to attract a passing migrant. After the birds know where a feeder is located, the red trim isn't necessary, but it is needed for newcomers. Red is so often the color of nectar-rich flowers, that most hummingbirds seem to know by instinct—or race memory or some other of nature's tricks—that red is the color to try. Meanwhile, if no hummers have found your syrup treat, check within a few days to see if it has started to ferment and show black spots. Rinse the feeder out carefully with plain water (no soap) and refill with fresh solution. When the hummers start coming regularly, you may need two or even three, each hung out of sight of the others so a different hummer can claim exclusive rights to each one.

Lately there has been discussion about the need to take in the feeders in the fall lest migrating hummers be tempted to linger beyond their natural food supply. Yet nature has not removed such temptation. Flowers are plentiful in mid-July and August when most northern males—with no nesting duties to detain them—start southward. Females and young usually wait until September, and they, too, leave flowers behind. The time for their departure is fixed by a pre-set inborn signal, not food supply. Usually the date is linked to day-length, and when the days are short enough, they will leave, no matter how abundant the food from either feeders or flowers. Only an injured bird not able to make the long flight, or some late hatchling not yet up to full strength will be likely to remain beyond the customary departure date. Even severe storms deter them only a few days or hours.

Anna's Hummingbirds, however, have no such pre-set signal, no inherited route of autumnal southern migration. Until recently almost the entire species has stayed year-round in southern California. When unusual cold or heat curtails their food supply, they wander down to warmer valleys or up to cooler hillsides as the weather prescribes, with seldom a need for far roving. In any year a few individuals may go on to Arizona, but there was no sizable exodus from southern California until the mid-1960s when persistent brush fires, floods and mud slides destroyed much of their feeding and nesting grounds. Those left hungry and homeless had no choice but to leave or perish. With arid desert lands on the south, the Pacific on the west, and eastward roving blocked by the Sierras, the easiest route was north through the valleys. And north they went.

Some of these northbound home-seekers went farther than might seem sensible to humans with an atlas in hand. But the Anna's had no such guidebook. Those that reached Oregon, Washington, and even more northern fields before nesting usually tried to stay there year-round in keeping with their inherited behavior pattern. A surprising number have succeeded over the ensuing years and it is their descendants who have triggered the current clamor to take down the syrup feeders on September 1st and "teach hummingbirds when to migrate."

Anna's Hummingbird by Lizars, from Jardine, Edinburgh, 1834.

Whether the Anna's will learn that lesson—or even need to—is a moot point. Food supply is the main factor in their survival, for hummingbirds as a family are expert at adapting to cold. Even in California, winter nights can be icy, yet the Anna's have gone about living as usual in temperatures as low as 25 degrees F. Their feathers provide remarkable insulation and they can torpidate by lowering their body metabolism to reduce the need for both warmth and food. In the wild they may also take night shelter in some cave or rocky crevice. In cities they are sometimes able to slip into a backyard greenhouse or other bulding with added warmth.

Other western hummers—the Broad-tailed, Calliope, and Rufous—have long nested high in the Rockies where temperatures even on summer nights can reach near-freezing. In the 1970s ornithologist William Calder tested over a hundred nests in Wyoming and Colorado. He found them so well insulated by their layers of down, fiber and cobwebs that the eggs under a brooding female could maintain a night temperature of 95-97 degrees F. even when the outside air registered only 46-79 degrees F. Anna's Hummingbirds could surely do the same.

However, they must eat, and winter syrup feeders have been an important factor in northern survival. But Anna's are experts at winter foraging. They probe sapsucker holes or fallen fir and pine cones for sap, find insect eggs and grubs on the ground or in crevices of trees and rocks, sip honeydew secretions left by aphids, leafhoppers snd their kin, seek out any remnants of pollen or nectar on half-frozen blossoms, find needed minerals in sandy soil or seeping spring water. One hummer even tried the suet put out for chickadees.

Lack of food—from either nature's store or syrup feeders—will certainly set northern Anna's to wandering, but it will not necessarily send them southward. After all, many of the Anna's now in the north are northern-born, not recent pioneers remembering a southern homeland in California. Keeping a winter feeder for hummingbirds or taking it down on September 1st is an individual decision, but the goal of teaching a non-migratory species to migrate at a set date doesn't seem part of the answer.

Some birdwatchers refuse to put out syrup feeders even in summer, insisting that only nature should provide. That, too, is an individual decision, and certainly the best way to welcome hummingbirds to the yard is with the flowers they like best. Their favorites, as Indian children learned long ago, are those richest in nectar. And since hummingbirds themselves are native Americans, it is not surprising to find that some of their flower favorites are of similar all-American origin. Fuchsias, a top favorite, originally grew wild from the Caribbean islands to Brazil and Chile. Europeans first heard of them in 1703 through a description in a French text by

Père Charles Plumier, who had discovered them in Santo Domingo. He named this plant to honor a long-dead German botanist, Leonhard Fuchs, and the name has remained in worldwide use. The first cuttings grown in Europe would not be on record until 1788 when a London nurseryman obtained a plant brought from Chile (or perhaps Brazil) by a young sailor. Shortly thereafter another species, definitely from Chile, was brought to London by another seaman, and other plants were taken to nurseries in the United States about this time.

Today, fuchsias come in many varieties and colors, but the hummingbirds prefer those most like the original wildlings—single blossoms of a bright red or pink color. Among favorites are the varieties Marinka, Red Spider, June Bride and Belle of Salem for hanging baskets and Gartenmeister, which grows upright and in some areas is winter hardy.

Other American flowers among the favorites are nasturtiums (native from Mexico to Chile), touch-me-not balsam or impatiens (native in eastern and midwestern U.S.), columbine, coral bells, trumpet creeper and petunias—all available almost everywhere in garden varieties. All garden petunias, by the way, are developed from two native wild plants from Argentina.

Individual birds often acquire favorites outside the typical listing, but a nationwide survey by *Bird Watchers' Digest* (May/June 1985) reported these five favorites: impatiens, fuchsia, honeysuckle, petunia and various salvia (sage) species. Authors Murphy and Dennis rated these next: azalea, bee balm, canna, geranium, Rose of Sharon and silk tree. Other watchers added locust, madrona, buddleia, nicotiana, red gilia and all the gooseberry-raspberry-currant clan.

When planning a garden to attract hummingbirds, you consider seasonal availability as well as abundance. Wild flowering currant and other early bloomers are of special importance to Northwest spring migrants. Late blooming flowers not troubled by late summer drought and heat are vital for the last southbound migrants. Your choices should be guided by hummingbird preference for pink, red or orange colors and single flowers of trumpet or tubular shape.

Hummingbird selection by shape and color is partly an inborn trait, partly learned from experience. As soon as the nestlings fledge, the mother customarily leads them to her own favorite nectar source and shows them by example how to use it. The youngsters usually get the idea at once and insert their own beaks for satisfying sips. But sometimes a fledgling is not so quick to understand the lesson and flutters about in bewilderment. On one such occasion watchers saw the mother sweep in beside the laggard, contorting her body at an almost incredible angle to avoid clashing wings, and insert her beak for repeat demonstrations. This time the youngster understood and was soon lapping up the syrup, torso arched, tail bobbing in typical hummer pose.

Identified as *Topaza pella*, by John Gould, London, 1861.

After brief example, fledglings are on their own, ready to learn from experience. You may see one land expectantly on a be-flowered patio chair cover, put its beak to the bright orange petals—and discover that shape and color are not always the real thing. Or they will try to reach through glass to probe an inside windowsill bouquet. Lipstick or a bright red cap, scarf or shirt may call for puzzled survey, too.

Hummers may even follow the gleaming tail light of a car right into the garage and then flutter above it in seeming amazement that anything so red and glowing has no nectar to offer.

The most dramatic proof that hummers use color clues came in the late summer of 1981 as migrant Rufous, southbound from Canada and Alaska, reached southern Washington. Mount St. Helens still stood sentinel there, as it had done some five hundred years—but not with the same rounded, snow-capped dome. This time the top was a gaping crater and to northward the land lay barren as moonscape, the aftermath of the massive volcanic eruption of May 18, 1980. Now, fifteen months later, a few plants had begun to struggle through ash and rock, a clump of fireweed here, a few stalks of lupin there, and straggling feelers of blackberry, elderberry, huckleberry in between.

Identified as *Lesbia victoriae*, by John Gould, London, 1861.

But not enough flowers to feed the host of migrants. And so on they went, some of them winging high enough above the rock-strewn desolation to look down over the crater's jagged rim to the ash-gray core far below. There geologists were setting out markers for the buried instruments that might give warning of future eruptions—each stake topped with a wind-tossed strip of bright red plastic.

The hummers saw those beckoning red strips and came diving down to bewildered frustration. No flower. Not even a bush where they might rest. One bird, perhaps more weary than the rest, settled for a moment on the arm of a geologist who crouched in motionless wonder, wishing the tiny visitor a silent godspeed.

HOW TO IDENTIFY HUMMINGBIRDS

Not so dramatic as the Mount St. Helens incident, but equally fascinating, are the times a hummingbird may come to splash in the misting spray of a hand-held garden hose. Back and forth it swings, a rainbow pendulum, granting a brief but incredibly close view of each color clue for certain identification—back, cap, throat, belly and tail.

Careful observers will make an identification check even in areas where only one hummingbird species is common. First make certain the nectar sipper is not a moth—most easily done by checking for the presence of a rigid bill. The moth has no bill. Its long tongue is flexible as it probes a flower and is coiled back against its mouth when not in use. The rigid hummer bill remains plainly seen as the bird flies to the next flower. Recognizing the hummingbird as unlike other small birds is the next step and usually easy. Any glimpse of that long bill and those whirring wings will do, as a twelve-year-old once proved with his amazed description of a bird that looked like "a cross between a baby sparrow and a darning needle."

Telling one hummingbird from another takes practice. Your chances for success are improved if you train yourself to follow a fixed pattern of clues and checkpoints—and make the sequence so automatic that you'll never have to watch a bird flit away while you're still wondering what clue to look for first.

Begin, then, by taking a flash-glance measurement of comparative size. Is the unknown hummingbird decidedly smaller than others you usually see? Or decidedly larger? Most hummer species are within the same 3- to 4-inch range, and so a decided difference either way could be a significant clue.

Next make a five-point color check. Look at the back first, then at the cap, throat, belly and tail—always in that sequence if possible. If the bird refuses to cooperate by turning full view, check the points you can see until you have them all or the bird flits. When it is no longer in view, match those five color points with pictures in your field guide. Match size, too, of course. Expect to see a species likely to be in your area, but don't rule out a rarity.

These days, when much of our own wildlands, and those in countries to the south of us, are being withdrawn from wildlife use by urbanization and increased agricultural or industrial sites, even hummingbirds are forced to look for new nesting and feeding grounds. In some areas much of former hummingbird territory is already lost to them, and chances are that more will be taken over as the years go on. The steady increase of rarities appearing all across the country proves that for hungry and homeless hummingbirds, there's a determined will to go pioneering if need be.

7.

NORTHERN RESIDENTS AND RARITIES

TWENTY-FOUR SPECIES of hummingbirds have been seen and identified in North America north of Mexico. Their presence has been verified by listing in *The AOU Check-list of North American Birds,* by reports in the magazine *American Birds* published by the National Audubon Society, from other reliable witnesses or with specimens collected as proof.

Sixteen of the twenty-four are presented here as 'residents' because of verified nesting records or because of repeated sightings during an entire season. The remaining eight are counted 'rarities' because they are seldom seen and only for brief visits. Five of these visitors are appearing with increasing frequency and may eventually become residents. The other three have only one verified northern sighting and will probably remain rarest of the rare. Of course, other rarities may appear at any time and any resident becomes a rarity outside its regular territory as far as local status is concerned.

Nevertheless, sixteen residents and eight rarities make up the present total for Order Apodiformes, Family Trochilidae north of Mexico, and resumés of these twenty-four follow. The genus to which each is assigned is indicated by the first word of the Latin binomial as explained in Chapter 5. Latin binomials listed in the headings are those of the *Check-list*, sixth edition. However, since the AOU considers the family under study for revision, variant scientific names in earlier widely-used texts are given, as are binomials recommended by two recent texts: *Hummingbirds of North America* by Paul Johnsgard and *Reference List of Birds of the World* by Morony, Bock and Ferrand.

Changes in nomenclature are certain to come in the future as they have in the past. But whatever the new scientific terms may be, hummingbirds are certain to remain "one of the wonders of the country" for all of us as they were for William Wood back in 1634.

The Residents

(To aid identification, resident species are grouped by key colors instead of the AOU classification sequence.)

KEY COLOR: RED THROAT (males)

Ruby-throated Hummingbird, from Ridgway, 1890.

Ruby-throated Hummingbird, *(Archilochus colubris)*
● Classification: First classified in 1758 as *Trochilus Colubris* by Linnaeus, one of the original species in his *Systema Naturae* and based on descriptions published by Mark Catesby and George Edwards. Re-classified in 1854 by Ludwig Reichenbach, director of the Dresden Zoological Museum. His *Archilochus* may honor a seventh-century Greek poet whose satire was as barbed as hummingbird belligerence. Or it could be from *archil,* Greek for 'purplish-red,' and *ochros* 'yellow.'
● Variant Names: As the only species in eastern North America, this was 'the' hummingbird of English colonists. 'Northern' and 'Red-throated' were used as modifiers before Audubon and Nuttall chose 'Ruby-throated.' Buffon listed it as *Le Rubis,* 'The Ruby.' In Mexico it is sometimes *chupamirto de*

fuego, 'myrtle-sipper color of fire.'
- Size: 3 to 3½ inches.
- Color Clues:* MALE: BACK green; CAP green; THROAT red; BELLY whitish; UNDERTAIL whitish; TAIL dark, notched. FEMALE: BACK green; CAP green; THROAT dotted on white; BELLY whitish; UNDERTAIL whitish; TAIL dark with green center feathers, notched, outer feathers tipped in white. CHECK: either sex may be confused with Broad-tailed when in same area in Mexico or on migration; however, the latter's tail is even, not notched.
- Range: Summers in eastern North America, not usually seen west of Great Plains except in Canada. Recent far-west sightings include Minot, South Dakota, 1984; Truckee, California, 1984; Crow's Nest Pass, British Columbia, 1983. Generally winters southern Mexico to Panama, occasionally in Florida or on the Gulf Coast and in West Indies. Winter sightings Key Largo and Coot Bay, Florida, and Port Aransas and Freeport, Texas, and New Orleans, Louisiana.

*Bills are dusky in color unless otherwise noted.

Broad-tailed Hummingbird, *(Selasphorus platycercus)*
- Classification: First classified in 1827 by British naturalist William Swainson as *Trochilus platycercus* (broad-tailed) from a specimen found in Mexico. Re-classified in 1832 in genus *Selasphorus,* 'torch-bearer.'
- Variant Name: No other common name. In Mexico it is *chupamirto de pecho color de carmine,* 'red breasted.'
- Size: 3¾ to 4½ inches.
- Color Clues: MALE: BACK green; CAP green; THROAT red; BELLY buffy-white; UNDERTAIL whitish; TAIL even tips, dark outer feathers. FEMALE: BACK green; CAP green; THROAT dotted on white; BELLY white, buffy sides; UNDERTAIL white V; TAIL center green, outer feathers rufous above black band, white tips. CHECK: *see* Ruby-throated.
- Range: Summers from Mexico north through Arizona, New Mexico into Rockies (Idaho, Colorado, Utah, Nevada, Wyoming) and Oregon, California. May wander eastward on migration, has wintered in Freeport and Buffalo Bayou, Texas.

Rufous Hummingbird, from Ridgway, 1890.

Rufous Hummingbird, *(Selasphorus rufus)*

• Classification: First classified in 1788 as *Trochilus rufus* by Johann Gmelin, German-born naturalist working in Russia, who based his description on the specimen collected in 1778 by Captain James Cook at Nootka Sound (Vancouver Island, BC). Second northern hummer on record. Re-classified by William Swainson.

• Variant Names: Listed as Ruff-necked Honey-sucker, Ruff-necked Hummingbird and Nootka Hummingbird by early writers. One Mexican Indian name meant 'bird of gold with throat of fire.'

• Size: 3½ to 3¾ inches.

• Color Clues: MALE: BACK cinnamon; CAP front green, rest cinnamon; THROAT fiery red, flares in ruff; BELLY white washed in rufous; UNDERTAIL mostly rufous; TAIL rufous with dark pointed tips. FEMALE: BACK green; CAP green; THROAT dotted on white, sometimes with small central red spot; BELLY washed in rufous; UNDERTAIL whitish V; TAIL center green, outer rufous with black band, white tips. CHECK: immature male easily confused with female and with adult male Allen's. Female Rufous and Allen's indistinguishable where ranges coincide.

• Range: Nests from northern California to Alaska and Yukon, Saskatchewan, Alberta, South Dakota. Winters in Mexico as a rule, wanders eastward in autumn. Has been seen in winter in Reserve, Lousiana, and in several Texas locations on the Gulf and inland to Houston and Austin, also Arkansas and Mississippi. In Ohio August 1985.

Allen's Hummingbird, *(Selasphorus sasin)*

• Classification: First classified in 1829 by French expert René Primevère Lesson as *Ornismya sasin* from a skin sent from California. Generic label coined by Lesson from Greek for 'bird-fly' (adapted from Oviedo's *pájaro mosca*). *Sasin* is Nootka Indian for hummingbird, first recorded by Captain James Cook in 1778 as applying to Rufous. Allen's does not normally share Nootka territory, and probably would not have been known to that tribe. Namesake is Charles Allen, Civil War veteran who went to California for his health in 1877 and was first American to define differences between this species and Rufous.

• Variant Name: In Mexico it is *petirrojo* (red breast-jewel), a name shared with the robins.

• Size: 3 to 3½ inches.

• Color Clues: MALE: BACK cinnamon on rump and nape, green on back and shoulders; CAP green; THROAT red; BELLY washed in cinnamon; UNDERTAIL mostly rufous; TAIL rufous with pointed black tips. FEMALE: BACK green; CAP green; THROAT dotted on white, may have small red center dot; BELLY washed in rufous; UNDERTAIL whitish V; TAIL center green, outer rufous with black band and white tips. CHECK: *see* Rufous.

• Range: Nests along California coast from Baja to southern Oregon. Winters in Mexico, occasionally in southern California (Palos Verdes, etc.).

Hybrid between Anna's and Rufous Hummingbirds, from Ridgway, 1890. (Labeled Floresi's Hummingbird in original.)

Anna's Hummingbird, *(Calypte anna)*

● Classification: First classified in 1829 by French expert René Lesson as *Ornismya anna* from a specimen brought from California by Dr. Paul Botta. Re-classified in genus *Calypte*, Greek for 'hood, cowl,' by British ornithologist John Gould in 1856. Johnsgard (1983) suggests re-classification in genus *Archilochus*. Lesson's specific name honors a Parisian beauty, Anne de Rivoli.

● Variant Name: In Mexico the name is *chupamirto de cabeza y cuello escarlata,* 'myrtle sipper with head and throat of scarlet.'

● Size: 3½ to 4 inches.

● Color Clues: MALE: BACK green; CAP (hood) red; THROAT red; BELLY grayish-green with white lower border; UNDER-TAIL mostly dusky; TAIL notched, outer feathers dark, center green. Only northern hummer with a red head. CHECK: male Costa's. FEMALE: BACK green; CAP green; THROAT usually with rather large central red spot; BELLY grayish-green; UNDERTAIL mostly grayish; TAIL green, outer feathers banded in black above white tips, no notch.

● Range: Formerly nested only in southern California, staying year-round except for occasional winter wanderers to Baja or Arizona or central California. No definite migration. Since loss of habitat in mid-60s has spread steadily north and east, usually seeking year-round home. By 1985 nesting and year-round resident in Arizona, Oregon, Washington, lower British Columbia. Seen with increasing frequency (and may soon nest) in Texas, New Mexico, Idaho, Colorado; less often in Montana, Utah, Nevada, Louisiana, Alaska; Sonora, Mexico; Alberta, Canada. (Alaska sightings since 1971 at least once in every month except April; 1 to 3 individuals; in Anchorage, Auke Bay, Cordova, Dillingham [July-October, 1984], Juneau, Ketchikan, Sitka, Wrangell.) Seen in Montana (Missoula) in 1969 but first sighting east of Continental Divide at Billings, Montana, Nov-Dec 1982. Major population still in southern California. Largest Audubon Society Christmas Bird Count usually from Santa Barbara (over 1,000); state total 5,000 to 8,000+; non-California total 325 to 457.

Calliope Hummingbird, from Ridgway, 1890.

Calliope Hummingbird, *(Stellula calliope)*

● Classification: First classified in 1847 by British expert John Gould as *Trochilus calliope* from a specimen found in Mexico. Re-classified in genus *Calothorax*, Greek for 'beautiful breast-plate,' by Gould and then in genus *Stellula*, 'little star.' Johnsgard (1983) suggests it belongs in genus *Archilochus*. Calliope was the name of the Greek muse of poetry, coined from *kalli*, 'beautiful' and *ope*, 'voice' or 'sound.' For this Calliope, the sound is wing music.

● Variant Name: In Mexico the Spanish name is *rafaguita*, 'little flashing sky beams,' and may refer to the streaked pattern of the gorget or simply to the effect of rapid flight and changing iridescence.

● Size: 2¾ to 3 inches; smallest bird nesting north of Mexico.

- Color Clues: MALE: BACK green; CAP green; THROAT purplish-red and white in flared striping; BELLY whitish, buffy at sides; UNDERTAIL white V; TAIL green, short, outer feathers dark. FEMALE: BACK green; CAP green; THROAT dotted; BELLY white, buffy at sides; UNDERTAIL whitish; TAIL green banded in black, outer tips white.
- Range: Nests from central California and Nevada north through western Oregon and Washington, Idaho, western Wyoming and Montana to Alberta and British Columbia. Seen at Crow's Nest Pass, BC in 1983. Normally winters in Mexico. Has been seen in winter in Ramsay Canyon, Arizona. Most common nesting hummer in Grand Teton National Park area, Wyoming.

KEY COLOR: PURPLE THROAT or CAP or HOOD (males)

Black-chinned Hummingbird, *(Archilochus alexandri)*
- Classification: First classified in 1846 as *Trochilus Alexandri* by French collectors Jules Bourcier and Martial Mulsant who had a specimen from Mexico. Re-classified by Ludwig Reichenbach of Dresden, Germany. Namesake *alexandri* honors a French doctor Alexandre who collected in Mexico in the 1840s and sent back several unknown birds—probably including this one—to Paris experts. 'Black-chinned' refers to the upper throat patch that does not change color, as does the lower purple patch.
- Variant Name: In Mexico it is known as *terciopelo barbanegro,* velvet blackbeard.
- Size: 3½ to 3¾ inches.
- Color Clues: MALE: BACK green; CAP green; THROAT black above, purple below; BELLY white; UNDERTAIL whitish V; TAIL dark, definitely notched. FEMALE: BACK green; CAP green; THROAT dotted faintly; BELLY white; UNDERTAIL whitish V; TAIL center green, outer dark tipped in white, no notch. CHECK: female not distinguishable from female Costa's.

- Range: Normally nests throughout U.S. Southwest, mid-Texas to the West Coast, with some individuals nesting north to eastern Oregon and Washington and southwest British Columbia. Has been seen in Alaska. Normally winters in Mexico. Has been seen in winter in Freeport, Texas, New Orleans and Reserve, Lousiana, Tucson Valley, Arizona, and San Diego, California, and five times in Florida near Tallahassee (1982-83). First for Alabama (Mobile, Spring Hill) November-April, 1984.

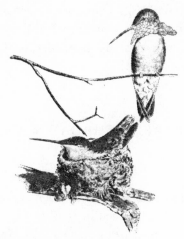

Costa's Hummingbird, from Ridgway, 1890.

Costa's Hummingbird, *(Calypte costae)*

- Classification: First classified in 1839 by French naturalist Bourcier in genus *Ornismya* (Lesson's term) after seeing a specimen from California. Re-classified in genus *Calypte* with Anna's because both have iridescent hoods, not just caps. Johnsgard (1983) suggests re-classification in genus *Archilochus*. Common and specific names honor Louis M. Costa, marquis de Beauregard, who was both professional diplomat and amateur naturalist.
- Variant Names: In Mexico it is *chupamirto de gola y cabeza violada,* violet-hooded. To one French writer it was Costa's moth-bird.
- Size: 3 to 3½ inches.
- Color Clues: MALE: BACK green; CAP (hood) purple; THROAT purple; BELLY white, greenish sides; UNDERTAIL

white V; TAIL green center, outer dark. FEMALE: BACK green; CAP green; THROAT white, faintly dotted, perhaps some purple; BELLY white; UNDERTAIL whitish V; TAIL center green, outer dark tipped in white. CHECK: female not distinguishable from female Black-chinned, unless purple throat spots can be seen at close range.

● Range: Nests in northwest Mexico and Baja, in eastern Arizona, southern California, extreme southern Nevada, southwestern Utah, Arizona, New Mexico; rarely in Oregon, British Columbia. Winters in southern portions of nesting range. Has been seen in winter in Hays County, Texas, and in Phoenix, San Diego, San Bernardino.

Magnificent (Rivoli's) Hummingbird, from Ridgway, 1890.

Magnificent (Rivoli's) Hummingbird, *(Eugenes fulgens)*
● Classification: First classified in 1827 by British naturalist William Swainson as *Trochilus fulgens,* 'refulgent hummingbird.' About the same time Lesson named it *Ornismya Rivoli* and two other French classifiers listed it as *L'Eugenes de Rivoli,* 'Rivoli's nobly-born one (or princeling)' honoring Francois Victor Massena, Duke of Rivoli and Prince of Essling and a noted collector of hummingbird skins for display in his Paris home. In 1856 John Gould resolved these

three labels into one, *Eugenes fulgens.* Johnsgard prefers to place it in genus *Heliodoxa* (sun worshipper) a term also coined by Gould for other species.

● Variant Names: Rivoli's was the official name until *The AOU Check-list* of 1983 changed it to Magnificent, a term used in early Mexican and British publications. In Mexico it is often called *chupamirto real,* 'royal myrtle-sipper,' or *verde montera,* which describes the green throat as appearing like light shining through a green glass window.

● Size: 4½ to 5 inches; next-to-largest seen in U.S.

● Color Clues: MALE: BACK green; CAP purple, white ear mark with black underline; THROAT jade green; BELLY dark green; UNDERTAIL grayish-white V; TAIL dark green, some gray tips. FEMALE: BACK green; CAP green, white ear mark with black underline; THROAT dotted; BELLY buffy; UNDERTAIL grayish; TAIL dark green, black bands above white tips. CHECK: both sexes much larger than similar White-eared Hummingbird.

● Range: Nests in southeastern Arizona, less often in Colorado, New Mexico, Texas. Nests and winters in Mexico. Has been seen in Utah. Has wintered in Arizona in Green Valley, Madera Canyon and Ramsay Canyon. First for California (Kern County) April 24, 1984.

White-eared Hummingbird, from Ridgway, 1890. (Labeled Xantu's Hummingbird in original.)

White-eared Hummingbird, *(Hylocharis leucotis)*

- Classification: First classified in 1818 by French expert Jean Louis Pierre Vieillot as *Trochilus leucotis* (white-eared) from a specimen tagged 'from Brazil' but later found to be from Vera Cruz, Mexico. Re-classified in genus *Hylocharis* (woodland beauty). Johnsgard (1983) suggests putting in genus *Cynanthus.*

- Variant Name: Many hummer species have small white ear marks, but those for this species are so prominent a clue that it has no other common names. In Spanish also it is *oreji-blanco,* 'white-eared.'

- Size: 3 to 3½ inches; much smaller than male Magnificent which also has a purple cap.

- Color Clues: MALE: BILL red tipped in black; BACK green; CAP purple, white ear mark underlined in black; THROAT purple directly under bill, rest bright green; BELLY yellowish green; UNDERTAIL grayish V; TAIL greenish gold. FEMALE: BILL red tipped in black; BACK green; CAP green, prominent white ear mark underlined in black; THROAT dotted; BELLY whitish, sides splotched in green; UNDERTAIL grayish V; TAIL green, outer tips white.

- Range: Normally nests in Mexco. Seen repeatedly in nesting season in Arizona (Portal, Madera Canyon, Chiricahua and Huachuca Mountains) and New Mexico (Animas Mountains) and Texas (Big Bend) and has stayed through October. First U.S. nest July 13, 1985, Portal, Arizona.

Lucifer Hummingbird, from Ridgway, 1890.

Lucifer Hummingbird, *(Calothorax lucifer)*
- Classification: First classified in 1827 by British naturalist William Swainson from a Mexican specimen he named *Cynanthus lucifer,* 'Little Bluish Light-bearer.' *Anthus* is Greek for 'bright' also for 'small bird,' so could be used as a diminutive; *cyn* is Greek for 'blue.' Re-classified in genus *Calothorax,* Greek for 'beautiful breasted.'
- Variant Names: William Bullock, a British traveler in Mexico in 1824, said its name in the local Indian language meant 'beams (or rays, locks, tresses) of the sun.' It is also known in Spanish as *morado grande,* 'great purple one' (*great* referring to large size of ruff, not bird). French classifiers labeled it *barbe bleu,* 'blue beard,' although the throat ruff is definitely more purple than blue. Gould called it Mexican Star.
- Size: 3¼ to 3¾ inches.
- Color Clues: MALE: BACK green; CAP green, small white ear mark underlined in black; THROAT brilliant purple, flares; BELLY grayish, greenish at sides; UNDERTAIL white V; TAIL green center, outer darker, definitely forked. FEMALE: BACK green; CAP green, white ear mark; THROAT buffy; BELLY buffy; UNDERTAIL whitish; TAIL green, rufous touches above

black bands and white tips—is *not* notched. CHECK: only northern hummer with down-curved bill.
- Range: Normally lives year-round in Mexico. Has been seen in Arizona, New Mexico, Texas. Has nested in Chisos Mountains, Texas, and in Chiricahua and Huachuca Mountains, Arizona.

Violet-crowned Hummingbird, *(Amazilia violiceps)*
- Classification: Formerly thought to be first classified in 1830 by German naturalist W. Deppe as *Trochilus verticalis* (crowned). Re-classified as *Amazilia verticalis* until 1983 when the AOU certified that Deppe had described a different species. The first valid classification was by John Gould in 1859 as *Cyanomyia violiceps,* 'violet-headed blue-fly.' The 1983 *Check-list* revised this to *Amazilia violiceps,* but the specific name may be revised again because it is already in use for the Violet-capped Hummingbird, *Goldmania violiceps,* and repeating a specific term within a family is not usually approved. With the 1859 date now valid for first listing, this is the last northern species to be classified.
- Variant Name: In Mexico it is usually called *corona azul,* 'blue-crowned,' a better color match than violet in most lights. This color confusion also explains Deppe's error.
- Size: 3¾ to 4¼ inches.
- Color Clues: MALE and FEMALE: BILL red with dark tips; BACK brown with grayish-greenish overtone; CAP bluish-violet; THROAT white; BELLY white; UNDERTAIL white V; TAIL same as back color with darker shading near tips.
- Range: Majority of individuals reside year round in Mexico. Has nested in southeast Arizona (Patagonia) and in New Mexico (Guadalupe Canyon). Seen in Arizona (Madera Canyon, Douglas, Huachuca and Chiricahua Mountains.) and in California (Santa Paula, Ventura County). Has wintered in Tucson, Arizona.

KEY COLOR: BLUE THROAT (males)

Blue-throated Hummingbird, from Ridgway, 1890.

Blue-throated Hummingbird, *(Lampornis clemenciae)*
● Classification: First classified in 1829 by René Lesson as *Ornismya clemenciae* from a specimen taken in Mexico. Specific name honors Lesson's wife, an artist known for her paintings of birds and flowers. French collectors Mulsant and Verreaux listed it as *Coeligne de Clemence* (Clemence's heavenborn one). Re-classified in genus *Lampornis* (lamp bird or torch bird).
● Variant Names: Gould found it known as Blue-throated Cazique *(casique, cacique* Taino for 'chieftain, king'). In Mexico its Spanish name means 'royal hummingbird with heavenly blue breast.' It was probably the Rain Bird of the Pimas.
● Size: 4½ to 5½ inches; largest northern hummer.
● Color Clues: MALE: BACK gray-green; CAP gray-green, white ear mark underlined in black and white; THROAT blue; BELLY greenish-gray; UNDERTAIL grayish V; TAIL blue, outer tail tips white (larger than white tips on other species). FEMALE: BACK gray-green; CAP gray-green, white ear mark underlined in black; THROAT grayish; BELLY grayish; UNDERTAIL grayish; TAIL blue with outer white tips.
● Range: Normally nests in Mexico and in southeastern Arizona, southern New Mexico and Texas. Has nested in southern California. Has wintered in Portal, Arizona. Wanders on migration. Has been seen in Springdale, Utah.

Broad-billed Hummingbird, from Ridgway, 1890. (Labeled Circe Hummingbird in original.)

Broad-billed Hummingbird, *(Cynanthus latirostris)*
- Classification: First classified in 1827 by British naturalist William Swainson from a specimen taken in Mexico. *Cyn* is Greek for 'blue'; *anthus* for 'bright' or 'small.' Specific name means 'broad-billed.' Swainson's original binomial is retained, although Gould suggested placing it in genus *Circe* in 1875, and in 1879 D.B. Elliott of the Smithsonian placed it in genus *Iache,* an alternate name for the Greek god of wine, Dionysius, as if to hint that this species sipped nectar as avidly as the god did wine.
- Variant Name: In Mexico it is *la matraquita,* 'little rattle shaker,' comparing the sound of its chirps or vibrating wings to that of the gourds shaken by medicine men during the Rain Dance ceremony.
- Size: 3¼ to 4 inches.
- Color Clues: MALE: BILL red tipped in black; BACK green; CAP bluish green, small white ear mark; THROAT peacock blue-green; BELLY peacock blue-green, slightly darker than throat; UNDERTAIL white V; TAIL dark blue, notched; immature males have small white tail tips. FEMALE: BILL red with black tip; BACK green; CAP green, white ear mark; THROAT grayish; BELLY grayish; UNDERTAIL grayish V; TAIL green, outer white tips, not notched. CHECK: female's ear

153

mark smaller than White-eared female's, also has no spotting on flanks as does the White-eared female.

- Range: Nests in Mexico and U.S. from southern Arizona to Texas. Winters in Mexico. Has been seen in central Arizona, central and southern California (Rancho Santa Fe, San Diego, Goleta, and San Marcos Pass near Santa Barbara), Springdale, Utah, Pensacola, Florida, and most recently in Seneca, South Carolina (July, 1985) and Alamo, Nevada (September, 1985).

KEY COLOR: GREEN HOOD, BUFF BELLY (both sexes)

Buff-Bellied Hummingbird, *(Amazilia yucatanensis)*
- Classification: First classified in 1845 as *Trochilus yucatanensis* by Dr. Samuel Cabot of Boston who spent much time birding in Central America and found this species in Yucatan.
- Variant Names: John Gould listed it as Fawn-breasted Hummingbird, but the diagnostic color is below the breast line. In Mexico it is called *vientro castana*, 'chestnut bellied,' but buff or fawn is a more accurate description.
- Size: 4 to 4½ inches.
- Color Clues: MALE and FEMALE: BILL red with dark tip; BACK green; CAP (hood) green; THROAT green; BELLY buff shading to whitish; UNDERTAIL buffy V; TAIL and rump cinnamon, tail feathers with darker tips, tail notched. CHECK: much like Berylline male and female but slightly larger, with paler belly. Lacks purplish rump tone of Berylline and has tail slightly more notched. See Berylline CHECK and Color Clues; also Rufous-tailed.
- Range: Normally year-round in Mexico; some individuals winter regularly in Texas (Armand Bayou, Brownsville, Corpus Christi, Freeport, Houston, Aransas, Santa Ana NWR). Has been seen in Louisiana (Baton Rouge, Franklin, New Orleans) every fall and winter since 1974. Seen near Pensacola, Florida, November, 1982. Nests Kingsville and Falfurrias, Texas, 1984.

Berylline Hummingbird, *(Amazilia beryllina)*

● Classification: First classified in 1830 as *Trochilus berylli-nus* by Martin Lichtenstein, founder of the Berlin Zoo, from a specimen taken in Mexico. Re-classified in genus *Amazilia* (literally 'little Amazonian,' but implying any South American tropics.) It is named for the gem of a similar blue-green color.

● Variant Name: In Mexico it is also known as *coli-canela*, 'cinnamon-tailed,' giving another color clue.

● Size: 3½ to 3¾ inches.

● Color Clues: MALE: BILL underpart has reddish tone; BACK glittering green at top shading to cinnamon and purple on rump and tail; CAP (hood) glittering green, comes well down on nape and breast; THROAT glittering green; BELLY dusky brown; UNDERTAIL cinnamon V; TAIL purpled cinnamon, notched. CHECK: similar to Buff-bellied but smaller, with darker belly, tail has purplish gloss which Buff-bellied lacks. Only lower part of bill is reddish, while entire bill of Buff-bellied is red. FEMALE: similar to male, though hood is not so far down onto breast and belly is brown, less dusky. CHECK: similar to female Buff-bellied, with same bill difference as for males. Also check Rufous-tailed.

● Range: Normally year-round in Mexico. Has been seen regularly in summer in southeastern Arizona (Ramsay Canyon) since 1967; three nesting records since 1976. Other Arizona sightings include Carr Canyon, Cave Creek Canyon, Garden Canyon, Portal, Madera Canyon, Chiricahua National Monument: June to September.

The Rarities

(To aid identification, species are grouped by area and frequency of U.S. sightings: two from the Southeast; three from the Southwest; three seen only once, east or west.)

SOUTHEAST

Bahama Woodstar, *(Calliphlox evelynae)*

- Classification: First classified in 1847 by French collector Jules Bourcier as *Trochilus Evelynae* from a bird he found in Nassau. The specific name presumably honors his wife. Reclassified in genus *Calliphlox*, Greek for 'beautiful flame.' Johnsgard (1983) suggests re-assigning to genus *Calothorax* and Morony (1975) placed it in genus *Philodice*, Greek for 'talk-loving' or 'cave-loving.'
- Variant Name: In the Bahamas it is still known as God Bird, one translation of the old Taino-Carib word *colibrí.*
- Size: 3½ to 3¾ inches.
- Color Clues: MALE: BACK green; CAP green with purple visor mark, white ear mark; THROAT brilliant purple shading to violet-blue with white bib border; BELLY cinnamon with greenish flanks; UNDERTAIL cinnamon to whitish; TAIL center green, glossed at edges with purple and cinnamon, deeply forked. CHECK: could be mistaken for a Rufous/Rubythroat cross unless purple tone of gorget is seen in good light. FEMALE: BACK green; CAP green with buffy visor mark; THROAT buffy white; BELLY cinnamon (paler than male's); UNDERTAIL buffy to rufous; TAIL buffy to rufous banded in dark purplish tone with lighter tips, not notched.
- Range: Resident through the Bahamas. Has appeared in Florida as visitor since 1961, most often around Miami and Homestead, in January, April, May, July, August, October. Seen at Mary Krome Memorial Bird Sanctuary just north of Homestead July 17-August 24, 1982, for one of its longer visits.

Cuban Emerald, *(Chlorostilbon ricordii)*

• Classification: First classified in 1835 by French collector Paul Gervais from a specimen taken in Santiago, Cuba. His label *Ornismya ricordii* honors French-American naturalist Philippe Ricord, born in Baltimore, Maryland. Re-classified in genus *Chlorostilbon,* 'green and glittering,' an apt color match.

• Variant Names: Sometimes listed as Ricord's Hummingbird. In Cuba and the Bahamas it is known by usual names— *colibrí, zunzun, zumbador, picaflor.*

• Size: 4 to 4½ inches.

• Color Clues: MALE: LOWER BILL pinkish; BACK metallic golden-green; CAP same green, white ear mark; THROAT same green; BELLY same green; UNDERTAIL white V; TAIL center dark green, outer feathers black, well notched. FEMALE: similar to male with metallic golden-green BACK and CAP, white ear mark; THROAT grayish; BELLY grayish, metallic green flanks; UNDERTAIL dark with white tufts; TAIL dark with violet overtone, notched.

• Range: Resident on Cuba, Isle of Pines, most northern Bahama Islands, rare on New Providence. Occasional visitor in southern and central Florida since 1961, especially in Dade County (August to November or January to March). On Hilton Head Island, South Carolina, September, 1981 (first sighting north of Florida).

SOUTHWEST

Plain-capped Starthroat, *(Heliomaster constantii)*

• Classification: First classified in 1843 by French naturalist Henri De Lattre from a specimen taken in Costa Rica. His binomial *Ornismya Constantii* honored a French author. Now re-classified in genus *Heliomaster,* 'sun pilot' (or chieftain, leader, master).

• Variant Names: Constant's Starthroat. In Spanish it is known both as *ocotero* (one who frequents the *ocotillo* flowers) and as *pochotero* (faded)—the latter because its plumage is not so bright as that of other species.

• Size: 4 to 4½ inches.

- Color Clues: MALE and FEMALE: Back metallic brownish-green; Cap duller brownish-green, white ear mark and drooping whisker mark; Throat dusky with bright red central spot (but not flaring gorget); Belly grayish shading to paler tone; Undertail gray with white edging, white V; Tail dusky, all but two central feathers tipped broadly in white.
- Range: Mexican resident year-round. Seen in Arizona since 1969 from Nogales to Phoenix and on to Sycamore Canyon, Sierra Vista, Patagonia, Madera Canyon, and also Copper Canyon, New Mexico.

Rufous-tailed Hummingbird, from Ridgway, 1890. (Labeled Rieffer's Hummingbird in original.)

Rufous-tailed Hummingbird, *(Amazilia tzacatl)*
- Classification: First classified in 1833 as *Trochilus tzacatl* by Pablo De La Llave, a physician-naturalist who collected in Mexico and classified several species. The specific name is from the Nahuatl language of the Aztecs, a variant of *tozcatl*, one of twelve names for hummingbirds recorded by Sahagún (See Chapter 4) with the comment: "It is ashen-colored at the top of its head; the throat feathers gleam like fire. They glisten; they glow." The Aztecs had taken over this term from the Toltecs, for whom it named a spirit-being who appeared as a hummingbird.
- Variant Names: Known as Rieffer's Hummingbird until 1983 *Check-list*, honoring the German naturalist who had shown De La Llave the specimen used for classifying. Mexicans call it *coli-rufo*, 'red-tail' or 'rufous tail,' or *pechi-gris*, 'gray-breasted.'

- Size: 4 to 4½
- Color Clues: MALE and FEMALE: BILL red with dark tips (upper bill often all dark); BACK green; CAP dusky green with dusky ear mark; THROAT glittering green with bluish overtone on down over breast; BELLY gray, sides green; UNDERTAIL cinnamon; TAIL rufous, slightly notched. CHECK: may be confused with Berylline and Buff-bellied, but cap is dusky green whereas theirs are bright green, and they lack so plain a dark ear mark. Also Berylline has dark bill.
- Range: Resident in Mexico and on south to Panama. First seen in U.S. at Ft. Brown (now Brownsville), Texas in 1876. Still seen occasionally at Brownsville and La Porte.

Green Violet-ear, *(Colibri thalassinus)*
- Classification: First classified in 1827 by William Swainson as *Trochilus thalassinus* from a species taken in Mexico. The specific name is Greek for 'sea green,' a reminder of the bird's blue-green brilliance. Re-classified in genus *Colibri*, the Taino-Carib word for 'hummingbird.'
- Variant Names: In Mexico it is *pavito*, 'little peacock.' In Venezuela it is *tucusito*, 'little firefly bird.'
- Size: 4¼
- Color Clues: MALE and FEMALE: female may be duller; BACK bright green; CAP somewhat darker green, large blue ear mark; THROAT green-blue; BELLY green; UNDERTAIL green V; TAIL blue crossed by darker band, blue-green feather tips.
- Range: Nests from Mexico south to Bolivia. First seen in Texas in July, 1961 (Santa Ana NWR) and since then in several areas (Hays, Hidalgo, Cameron, Travis, and Brazoria counties, and Padre Island) from April through September. Also seen Kern County, California, and Fort Smith, Arkansas (October 1985).

Single Sighting

Mango, *(Anthracothorax, species uncertain)*
- Classification: Linnaeus classified the Jamaican Mango as *Trochilus Mango* in 1758 and the Antillean Mango as *Trochilus dominicus* in 1766. Five other Mango species were

classified by later naturalists. Audubon also described and pictured a Mango which he believed was the species first named by Linnaeus. However, Audubon's original label was Mangrove Hummingbird (#184) and later ornithologists have not agreed on which Mango species he saw. It is certain that he had a specimen in hand, a bird seen alive in Key West, Florida, by a friend prior to 1840. It is also certain that no Mango has been reported in U.S. to the AOU or *American Birds* since that time.

● Size: Audubon listed 4¾ inches. Jamaican and Antillean Mangos are 4½ to 5 inches.

● Color Clues: The name may have been chosen to indicate the shade of green basic to Mango coloring. Or the first bird so named had a preference for nesting or feeding among West Indies mango trees, introduced from Asia by early colonists.

Identified by Ridgway as Guerin's Helmet-crest *(Oxypogon Guerini)*, 1890.

Bumblebee Hummingbird, *Atthis heloisa.*
● Classification: First classified in 1839 by French naturalists René Lesson and Henri De Lattre from a specimen taken in Mexico, with binomial *Ornysmya Heloisa*—the name probably honoring De Lattre's wife. However, since the classifiers did not state the namesake, it might have been the eleventh-century French nun famous for her beautiful love letters to Abelard, the lover she could not wed. The generic name is Greek, perhaps a misprint for *actis,* 'sunbeam.' Or it could be a variant spelling for Athenian, thus comparing this species to the nightingale, sometimes known as the Athenian bird,

because *heloisa* is one Trochilid with a real song. Males often sing together from nearby perches in a little whistly tune lasting half a minute or so. Johnsgard (1983) places it in genus *Selasphorus*.

• Variant Names: British expert John Gould called it Heloisa's Flame Bearer. In some texts it is Heloise's Hummingbird or Morcom's Hummingbird, honoring G. Frean Morcom who found two females in Huachuca Mountains of Arizona July 2, 1876 for first and only U.S. record to date.

• Size: 2½ to 2¾ inches. If residence in U.S. is established, it would tie with Calliope as smallest U.S. species.

• Color Clues: MALE: BACK bronze-green; CAP bronze-green; THROAT magenta to purple; BELLY whitish; UNDERTAIL white V edged in rufous; TAIL bronze-greeen with rufous overtone, white tips.

• Range: Resident Mexican highlands. One sighting in Arizona, Huachuca Mountains, July 2, 1876.

Antillean Crested Hummingbird, *(Orthorynchus cristatus)*

• Classification: First classified in 1758 by Linnaeus as *Trochilus cristatus,* based on description of English naturalist George Edwards of a specimen taken on Barbados. The generic name means 'straight-billed' and the specific name means 'crested'—matching the jaunty topknot.

• Variant Names: The French name *huppé* also means 'crested' but French-speaking settlers in the West Indies also call it *frou-frou,* a rustling word to echo the wing whir. In the Lesser Antilles it is Little Doctor Bird. The Spanish *zumbadorcito,* 'little hummer,' is also heard.

• Size: 3½ to 4 inches.

• Color Clues: MALE: BACK dark bronze-green; CAP and crest flare bright green with longer feathers shading to bluish tones; THROAT grayish; BELLY darker gray; TAIL black with glossy overtones of purplish bronze. FEMALE: similar, but lighter-toned and lacks crest.

• Range: Various Caribbean islands from eastern Puerto Rico to Barbados and Grenada. Indivudal seen in Galveston, Texas, February, 1967, may or may not have been an escaped cage bird. No further sightings to date.

The story of the hummingbirds—their history, their many mysteries and their link with myth and magic—has some chapters that are complete. But others may never be finished as long as there are hummingbirds on the wing and people to watch them in awe and wonder, and with questions not yet fully answered.

Among such questions are these: Will the Anna's Hummingbirds establish a regular annual north-south migration route? Or will they learn to survive in the north in increasing numbers? Or will they vanish from all but southern areas? What else will science discover about the role of torpidation for hummingbirds and other species? Will increasing loss of wild lands send still more tropical and semi-tropical species northward? Will we be seeing more rarities—and more rarities that turn into residents? Or fewer hummingbirds of any kind? Will depleted populations of certain hummingbird species throughout the Americas diminish to the point of extinction? Or will the last survivors interbreed with closely related species and so beget races of hybrids that may—or may not—eventually become established as full species? How many more species of hummingbirds are still to be discovered?

You may seek other legends and additional names for hummingbirds besides those listed here. And it is a continuing challenge to find more travel diaries and explorers' journals with pictures and descriptions of first sightings.

Yet almost all of us, at least some of the time, will watch hummingbirds with no questions in mind at all but only joy and wonder in the watching. Like the Indians of old, we feel a hint of mystery and magic with every fluttering wingbeat. Like Oviedo, we would scarcely dare talk about their elfin size and jewel colors without the assurance that many others watch and marvel, too.

8.

A Sampling Of Indian Names For Hummingbirds

In the beginning almost every tribe from Alaska to Tierra del Fuego must have had some name for hummingbirds, since they were seen throughout the hemisphere for at least part of each year. And in the beginning each of these names had a meaning—an echo of the humming wing whir or some reference to the bird's small size, brilliantly reflective colors, unique flying skills or their role in tribal legends.

By the time Europeans heard these ancient names and tried to reproduce them with phonetic syllables, many names had already collapsed—as words tend to do with centuries of careless usage—and no longer kept all the syllables of the original term to make the meaning clear. Like the English phrase 'God be with you!' that collapsed over the years to 'goodby,' many Indian names have lost all but a trace of the word as it was first spoken. Even Indians of today may not know the original term or its meaning, and so the word has become just one more hummingbird mystery.

Trying to solve such word-mysteries is worthwhile, for those ancient words reveal what the Indians knew of hummingbird ways—or what they believed they knew—and what they held important for namesake coinage. A search for names and meanings is part of hummingbird history, and leads to the fascinating study of old diaries and tribal vocabularies compiled in centuries past by travelers and traders, missionaries, historians, ethnologists and anyone else who took the time to write down what was learned in daily exchange or persistent questioning.

That search is far from complete. Often quite different translations have been recorded for the same word, or different names for hummers used by the same tribe. Often no meanings are given at all—just the words in phonic syllables as they sounded to alien ears or as they are known to tribal members. Here is a sampling from the many that could be charted if all were known. Though these names are only a partial tally, they are full witness to the value of written records in a search for an understanding of hummingbird ways.

NAMES CARRYING A PHONETIC ECHO OF WING SOUND
Aztec: *Zunzon, Cinçoni*
Chinook: *Etsentsen, Tsentsen*
Maidu: *Humpilisto*
Maya: *Dzunuum, Tznuum, Zumzum*
Nootka: *Sasin, Sasinne*
Quileute: *Tsibiba-atsit*
Tarascon: *Tsintsun, Zinzin, Cinçoni*
Yakima: *Hmamsa, Xmamsa*

NAMES LINKED TO LEGENDARY ROLES
Arawak: *Yee-ay, E-ay* (Sky Spirit, Nectar Bird, Bee-like)
Cherokee: *Tsa-lu Tsi-skwa* (Tobacco Bird)

Navaho: *Da-hi-tu-hi* (One Who Brings Life)

Taino/Carib: *Colibrí* (God Bird, Sky Spirit, Sun-God Bird—used especially for Cuban Emerald, Bahama Woodstar and Vervain Hummingbird)

Toltec: *Tozcatleton, Tezcatleton, Tzactl* (Little Rain Bringer, Little Life Giver)

Warrau-Carib: *Pisai* (Tobacco or Medicine Bird)

NAMES DESCRIBING APPEARANCE

Aymara: *Quendi, Quenti, Quinte, Quinti-ut* (Sun-gilded)

Aztec: *Huitzili, Huitzitzil, Uitzitzil* (Shining One with the Weapon [i.e. beak] Like a Cactus Thorn. Some translators use Shining One on the Left [or From the South] as part of the basic meaning. This word was combined with descriptive modifiers for certain species: *Chalchi-* for 'jade colored,' *Itztoc-* for 'white,' *Quetzal-* for 'precious,' *Nex* for 'ash-colored,' *Quiau-* for 'rain-bringing,' *Tenoc-* for 'prickly-pear cactus,' *Tozcacos-* for 'yellow-collared,' *Xiu-* for 'turquoise-colored,' *Zochio-* for 'multi- colored' or 'flower-like,' *Tlil-* for 'black-winged' or 'black- tailed.')

Kwakiutl: *K-waak-umtia* (Bird with Face Painted by Sun)

Maya: *Xo-ma-xamil* (Many Colored, Bird of Gold with Throat of Fire)

Miwok: *Li-ci-ci-nt* (Calliope Hummingbird, One With [or Like] a Strawberry)

Omaha: *Wati-ninika-wahize-nga* (Bird Like a Butterfly)

Pima: *Vipisimal* (Little Long Beak)

Tupi: *Aratica, Arataraguarci* (Possibly means 'Curved Beak' since similar words named toucans, parrots, scarlet ibis—all with curved beaks, as are some hummers. Perhaps it was such a hummer that led Sir Walter Raleigh to say he had seen "parakeets smaller than wrens" along the Orinoco River.)

NAMES DESCRIBING ACTIONS

Abnaki: *Nana-tas-is* (The Hoverer)

Aymara: *Nouna, Nouna-koali* (Striker, Club Wielder, Fighter)

Aztec: *Tsi-tsi-totol* (Bird That Says 'tsi-tsi'), *Vicisilin, Viemalin, Vitzitzili* (Reborn One, Returns-to-Life Bird. A basic word combined with modifiers for certain species: *Tle-* for 'fire-colored' and *Yiauh-* for 'with the rain.'

Chinook: *Au-puetts-inne, O-poots-in-a-ti* (One Who Goes Tail First)

Delaware (Canadian): *Li-li-tcas, Mi-li-tcas* (Smeller of Flowers)
Hopi: *Totca, Tocha, Totsa* (Bee-like One)
Makah: *Kwe-ta-kootch, Quitakootch* (They Suck Sweet Water) and
    Kwi-teeksitsch (They Dash and Dart, Stop and Go Suddenly)
Malacite: *Yalamés-it* (The Hoverer)
Michoacán: *Vicisiln* (Reborn One)
Navaho: *Da-hi-tu-hi* (One Who Brings New Life) and *Tsi-ke-*
    nazili (One Who Rattles)
Nitinot: *Ka-ka-wa-cik* (They Bring [Make] Salmon Berries)
Penobscot: *Ana-tás-is* (The Hoverer)
Tupi: *Guainumbi, Guanimbi, Guanambi,* and possibly *Gonam-*
    buch (Those Who Frequent the *Guanambaño* Tree, or, per-
    haps, echoic)
Zuñi: *Tanya* (Bee-like One)

NAMES WITH MISCELLANEOUS MEANINGS
Narragansett: *Sachem* (Chieftain, King, Leader)
Taino: *Cacique, Casique, Cazique* (Chieftain, King, Leader)
Tribe not cited, Brazil: *Ourissia* (Sunbeam, Rays of the Sun)
Tribe not cited, Venezuela: *Tucoso, Tucosito* (Firefly, Little Firefly,
    the 'ito' ending is Spanish diminutive added to Indian
    name.)

NAMES RECORDED WITHOUT LITERAL MEANING
Apache: *Dat-il-ye*
Arapaho: *Hati-ku-tha*
Chehalis: *Der-chee'to-che-nay*
Karoc: *Hou-pu-chee naish-wen*
Keresan: *Mi-itsr*
Klamath: *Pis*
Menomini; *Na-na-tska*
Micmac: *Miledow*(Beautiful?)
Mixtec: *Dee-yoo, Dilloo*
Nisqually: *Ta-had*
Ojibway: *Na-nooskau-see*
Wintu: *Lutchi-heret* (cf. Miwok *Li-ci-ci-nt*)
Yurok: *Tse-ge-mem*

Zapotec: *Piqui-jni-peyp-lao*
Tribe not cited, Aruba, Curacao: *Blenchi, Blenchi hudiu*
Site unknown: *Pigada, Courbir*

SPECIES KNOWN TODAY AS 'DOCTOR BIRDS' IN LOCAL AREAS
Rufous-breasted Hermit, *Glaucis hirsuta.* From Panama to Brazil,
    known as Brown Doctor Bird.
Green-breasted Mango, *Anthracothorax prevostii.* From Mexico to
    Peru, known as Green Doctor Bird.
Jamaican Mango, *Anthracothorax dominicus.* Jamaica.
Antillean Mango, *Anthracothorax jugularis.* Lesser Antilles.
Green-throated Carib, *Sericotes holosericeus.* West Indies.
Antillean Crested Hummingbird, *Orthorhynchus cristatus.* Lesser
    Antilles, known as Little Doctor Bird.
Streamertail, *Trochilus polytmus.* Jamaica, known as Long-tailed
    Doctor Bird.
Vervain Hummingbird, *Mellisuga minima.* Jamaica, known as
    Little Doctor Bird.

Although these names are only a partial tally, they are full
witness to the search for knowledge of hummingbird nature
that Amerind people have shared since ancient times. They
also testify to the worth of written records and to the challenge every tommorrow holds for all who seek to know the
way of the hummingbird.

Bibliography

Acosta, José de. *Naturall and Morall Historie of East and West Indies.* London: Edward Grimston, 1604. (Original, Seville: 1590.)

Alexander, H.B. *North American Mythology.* Boston: Marshall Jones Co., 1916.

American Birds. National Audubon Society, New York. Articles on distribution all issues. Christmas count. July-August isues.

American Ornithologists' Union. *Check-list of North American Birds.* Washington, D.C.: American Ornithologists' Union, editions 3-6, 1910, 1931, 1957, 1983.

Anderson, A.W. *How We Got Our Flowers.* New York: Dover Publications, Inc., 1966. (Original, London: Williams & Norgate, 1950.)

Arno Hermanos. *Catalogo de las Voces Usuales de Aimara, Castellano y Quechua.* La Paz, Bolivia: Arno Hermanos, 1944.

Audubon, John James. *Birds of America,* 7 vols. New York: Dover Publications, Inc., 1966. (Original, Audubon & Chevalier, 1840-44.)

Bacon, Peter R. "Hummingbirds drinking sea water." *Auk* 90:4, p. 917, October 1973.

Bakeless, John. *The Eyes of Discovery.* New York: Dover Publications, Inc., 1961. (Original, J.B. Lippincott, 1950.)

Barker, M.A.R. *Klamath Dictionary.* Berkeley: Univ. of Calif. Press, 1963.

Barker, Will. "Tales Once Told." *Birds in Our Lives,* Alfred Stefferud, editor. Washington, D.C.: Dept. of Interior, 1966.

Beall, Tom. *Legends of the Nez Perce.* (as told to R.D. Leper). Lewiston, Idaho: no date—reprinted from *Lewiston Morning Tribune,* various editions ca. 1935.

Beechey, Frederick W. *Narrative of a Voyage.* London: Colburn and Bentley, 1831.

Belon, Pierre. *L'Histoire de la Nature des Oyseaux.* Paris: Chez Guillaume Cavellat, 1555. (Microfilm S-22 Reel 11, French Books Before 1601.)

Bené, Frank. *The Feeding and Related Behavior of Hummingbirds.* Boston: Charles T. Branford, Co., 1942.

Benson, Elizabeth P. *The Maya World.* New York: Crowell, 1967.

Bent, Arthur Cleveland. *Life Histories of North American Cuckoos, Goatsuckers, Hummingbirds and Their Allies.* Washington, D.C.: U.S. National Museum Bulletin 176, 1940. Reprint, Dover. 1964.

Blunt, Wilfrid. *The Compleat Naturalist: A Life of Linneaus.* New York: Viking Press, 1971.

Boas, Frank. *Handbook of American Indian Languages.* Washington, D.C.: U.S. Government Printing Office, 1911.

Bond, James. *Birds of the West Indies.* Boston: Houghton Mifflin, 1980.

Bonney, Richard E. "Seeing Red." *Living Bird Quarterly* 3:25, Spring 1984.

Bowes, Anne L. *Birds of the Mayas.* (Folklore as told by Ramon Castillo Perez.) Big Moose, N.Y.: West-of-the-Wind Publications, 1964.

Broadbent, Sylvia. *South Sierra Miwok Language.* Berkeley: University of California Press, 1964.

Buffon, Georges, comte de. *L'Oiseau-Mouche* (in *Histoire Naturelle*). Paris: 1749-67.

Bullock, William. *Six Months Residence and Travels in Mexico. London: John Murray,* 1824.

Bunzel, Ruth. *Zuñi Katcinas.* Glorieta, N.M.: Rio Grande Press, 1973 (Reprint from U.S. Bureau of Ethnology Annual Report, 1929-30).

Calder, William. "Daylength and the Hummingbird Use of Time," *Auk* 92:1, January 1975.

—— "Energy Crisis of the Hummingbird," *Natural History* 85: 24-29, May 1976.

Cantwell, Robert. *Alexander Wilson*. Philadelphia and New York: J.B. Lippincott Co., 1961.

Casd Alfonso. *The Aztecs*. Norman, OK: University of Oklahoma Press, 1958.

Catesby, Mark. *Natural History of Carolina, Florida, and the Bahama Islands*. Savannah, GA: Beehive Press, 1974. (Fascimile of original, London: 1731, 1743, self-published.)

Clusius, Carolus (Charles de L'Ecluse). *Exoticorum Libri decem: quibus animalium, plantarum*. Antwerp: Officina Plantiana Raphelengi, 1605.

Colton, Harold S. *Hopi Kachina Dolls*. Albuquerque, NM: University of New Mexico Press, 1959.

Correll, Donovan S. "Vanilla, Its Botany, History, Cultivation and Economic Import." *Economic Botany* Oct.-Dec. 1953, 291-358.

Coues, Elliott. *Key to North American Birds*. Boston: Dana Estes & Co., fourth edition, 1903.

Curtis, Natalie. *The Indians' Book*. New York: Harper and Brothers, 1923. (Dover reprint, 1968.)

Dacos, Nicole. *Le Logge de Raffaello*. Rome: Instituto polifgrafico dello stato libreria, 1977.

—— "Présents Americains à la Renaissance." Paris: *Gazette de Beaux Arts* 6, LXXIII, pp. 57-64, Jan. 1969. Imprimerie Louis Jean, Gap, Switzerland.

Dance, S. Peter. *The Art of Natural History*. Woodstock, NY: Overlook Press, 1978.

De Angleria, Pedro Martir. *De Orbe Novo: The Eight Decades of Peter Martyr D'Anghera*. (Francis A. MacNutt, translator) 2 vols. New York: G.P. Putnam's Sons, 1912 (originally published Italy 1504, etc.; Spain 1511-30).

De Armas, Juan Ignacio. *La Zoología de Colón y de los Primeros Exploradores de América*. Havana, Cuba: Establecimiento Tipografico O'Reilly, 1888.

De Rosada, Engracia. *Birds Were Different Then*. San Diego, California: San Diego Schools Curriculum Project, 1936.

De Schauensee, Rodolphe and Phelps, W.H. *A Guide to the Birds of Venezuela*. Princeton, NJ: Princeton University Press, 1978.

Duhaut-Cilly, Auguste. *Voyage autour du Monde*. Paris: 1834-35. Translated by Roland Alden in *Early Naturalists in the Far West*. San Francisco: California Academy of Science, Occasional Papers, 1943.

Duran, Fray Diego. *Book of the Gods and Rites and Ancient Calendar*. Norman, OK: University of Oklahoma Press, 1971. Originally written in Spanish, Mexico, 1579.

Eden, Richard. *The Decades of the Newe Worle or West India*. London: Paul's Churchyard, 1555. (Translation of *De Orbe Novo* [see Angleria, Pedro Martir] and *Historia natural de las Indias* [see Oviedo, Gonzalo Fernández de] reprinted in facsimile.) New York: Readex Microprint Corporation, 1966. (Available on microfilm, W.L. Clements Library, University of Michigan, Ann Arbor, Michigan, American Culture Series.)

Ewald, Paul. "The Hummingbird and the Calorie." *Natural History* 88:92-98, 122, Aug./Sept. 1979.

Ewan, Joseph and Nesta. *John Banister and His Natural History of Virginia, 1678-1692.* Urbana, IL: University of Illinois, 1970.

Feduccia, Alan, ed. *Catesby's Birds of Colonial America.* Chapel Hill, NC: University of North Carolina Press, 1985. (Includes original text and pictures from Catesby's *Natural History of Carolina, Florida and the Bahamas.* London: 1732-43.)

Finger, Charles. *Tales from Silver Lands.* New York: Doubleday, 1924.

Fisher, Allan C. "Mysteries of Bird Migration." *National Geographic,* August 1979, pp.154-193.

Gill, Frank B. "Hummingbird Flight Speeds." *Auk* 102:97-101, January 1985.

Gesner, Conrad. *Historiae animalium lib III qi est de avium natura.* Zurich, Switzerland: 1555 and various subsequent editions.

Grant, Karen A. and Verne. *Hummingbirds and Their Flowers.* New York: Columbia University Press, 1968.

Greenwalt, Crawford. *Hummingbirds.* Garden City, NY: Doubleday, 1960.

_____ "The Hummingbird." *National Geographic,* Nov. 1960, p.675.

Hainsworth, F. Reed, and Wolf, Larry. "Regulation of Oxygen Consumption and Body Torpor in a Hummingbird." *Science,* vol. 168:368-9, April 1970.

Hainsworth, F. Reed. "To Feed a Hummingbird." (Letter to Editor) *Natural History,* 82:6-8, November 1973.

Harrison, T.P. "Longolius on Birds." *Annals of Science,* XIV:257-68, 1958.

Hernández, Francisco. *Cuatro libros de la naturaleza y virtudes medicinales de las plantas y animales y minerales de Nueva España usados en la medicina.* Mexico: 1615, 1888 (Latin original written ca. 1571-75) *Nova plantarum, animalium et mineralium mexicanorum Historia.* Roma: Typis Vitalis Mascardi, 1651.

Honour, Hugh. *The New Golden Land.* New York: Pantheon, 1975.

Howell, Donna J. "Plant-Loving Bats, Bat-Loving Plants," *Natural History,* 85:52-59, February 1976.

Inouye, David and Waser, N.M. "Broad-tailed Hummingbirds Banded in Colorado." *Auk* 94:393-5, April 1977.

Jagendorf, M.A. *Legends of Pitch Lake.* New York: Vanguard, 1960.

Jane, Cecil. *The Journal of Christopher Columbus.* New York: Bramhall House (Clarkson Potter), 1960.

Jardine, Sir William. *The Naturalists' Library.* vols. 6-7. London/Edinburgh: W.H. Lizars (no date, 1833-34).

Johnsgard, Paul. *The Hummingbirds.* Washington, D.C.: Smithsonian Institution Press, 1938.

Josselyn, John. *An Account of Two Voyages: 1638-39, 1663-71.* London: Widdowes, 1674. University Microfilms, Reel 980; English Books 1475-1640.

_____ *New Englands Rarities.* London: G. Widdowes, 1672. Reprint, Boston: William Veazie, 1865. University Microfilms, Reel 980.

Kalm, Pehr (Peter). *Travels in North America.* New York: Dover Publications, Inc., reprint 1966 (original Swedish publication, Stockholm, 1753; first English translation, John Reinhold Forster, 1770; revised, Adolph Benson 1937).

Kastner, Joseph. *A Species of Eternity.* New York: Dutton 1979.

Klimkiwicz, M.K.; Clapp, R.B., and Fuchter, A.G. "Longevity of North American Hummingbirds." *Journal of Field Ornithology* 54:123-137, 1983.

Kroeber, A.L. *Yurok Myths.* Berkeley, CA: University of California Press, 1976.

Krutch, Joseph. *World of Animals.* New York: Simon & Schuster, 1961.

L'Ecluse, Charles (see *Clusius, Carolus*).

Linnaeus, Carl. *Systema Naturae.* Tenth edition. Sweden: 1758.

Longolius (see Harrison, T.P.)

Lumden, James. *Animals.* Glasgow: James Lumden, 1794. Facsimile reprint, New York: Hudson River Press, 1977.

Lysaght, A.M. *The Book of Birds.* London: Phaidon Press Ltd., 1975.

Marcgrave, Georg. *Historia Naturalis Brasiliae.* Leyden, Amsterdam: 1648.

Matthews, Washington. *Navaho Legends.* Boston: Houghton-Mifflin for American Folklore Society, vol. 5, 1897.

Miall, L.C. *The Early Naturalists.* London: Macmillan, 1912.

Mera, H.P. *The Rain Bird: Pueblo Designs.* Santa Fe, NM: Laboratory of Anthropology, 1938. (Dover Publications reprint, 1970.)

Merory, Joseph. *Food Flavorings.* Westport, CT: Avi Publishing Co., 1968.

Monardes, Nicolas. *Las cosas que traen de nuestras Indias Ocidentales.* Sevilla: 1569. English translation: *Joyfull Newse out of the newe founde worlde* by John Frampton, London: 1577.

Montes de Oca, Rafael. *Hummingbirds and Orchids of Mexico.* Mexico DF: Editorial Fournier, 1963.

Morony, J.J.; Bock, W.J., and Ferrand, J. *Reference List of Birds of the World.* New York: American Museum of Natural History, 1975.

Morton, Thomas. *New English Canaan.* Amsterdam: J.F. Stam, 1637.

Murphy, Pat, and Dennis, John. "Feeding Hummingbirds." *Bird Watcher's Digest* 6:4 pp60-68; 7:4 pp28-36; 7:6 p6.

Newman, Cathy. "Pollen." *National Geographic,* October 1984, pp. 490-521.

Newcomb, Franc Johnson. *Navajo Folk Tales.* Albuquerque, NM: Museum of Navajo Ceremonial Art, 1967.

———— *Navajo Bird Tales.* Wheaton, IL: Theosophical Publishing House, 1970.

Orr, Robert T. *Animals in Migration.* New York: Macmillan, 1970.

Oviedo y Valdés, Gonzalo Fernández de. *De la Natural hystoria de las Indias.* Toledo, Spain: 1526.

Pearse, Theed. *Birds of the Early Explorers in the Northern Pacific.* Comox, British Columbia: Theed Pearse, 1968.

Pearson, Oliver. "Living Gems" (The University Explorer radio program), University of California, March 30, 1969.

Perry, Frances. *Flowers of the World.* London: Hamlyn Publishing Group, Ltd., 1972.

Powell, J.V. and Woodruff, Fred. *Quileute Dictionary.* Moscow, ID: Northwest Anthropological Research Notes, vol. 1, #1, part 2, 1976.

Prescott, William. *History of the Conquest of Mexico.* New York: Maynard, Merrell & Co., 1895. (Modern Library reprint undated.)

Prophit, Willie M. "Banding Hummingbirds." *Bird Watcher's Digest* 6:4, pp10-13.

Rand, Rev. S.T. *Dictionary of the Language of the Micmac Indians.* Halifax, NS: Nova Scotia Printing Co., 1888.

Ridgway, Robert. *The Hummingbird.* Washington, D.C.: Report of the U.S. National Museum, 1890 (reprint 1898).

Ruschi, Augusto. *Beija-flores do Estado do Espiritu Santo.* Sao Paulo, Brazil: Editorial Rios, 1982.

Sahagún, Bernardino de. *Historia General de Cosas de Nuevo España. Book 12.* Translated by C.E. Dibble and J.O. Anderson. Salt Lake City, UT, and Albuquerque, NM: Presses of the Universities of Utah and New Mexico, 1963 (written ca. 1560).

Saunders, George. *Honne, The Spirit of the Chehalis* (collected and published by Katherine Van Winkle Palmer). Geneva, NY: W.F. Humphrey Press, 1925.

Scheithauer, W. *Hummingbirds.* New York: T.Y. Crowell, 1966.

Schoolcraft, Henry R. *Schoolcraft's Indian Legends from Algic Researchers.* New York: Harper, 1839. Reprint: Michigan State University Press, 1956.

Shaw, Anne. *Pima Legends.* Tucson, AZ: University of Arizona Press, 1968¿

Shipley, W.F. *Maidu Texts & Dictionary.* Berkeley: University of California Press, 1963.

Skutch, A.F. *Life of the Hummingbird.* New York: Crown Publishers, 1973.

Smith, Charles. "Chickadees in Winter." *Bird Watcher's Digest,* Jan/Feb 1981, 11-13.

Smith, John Maynard. "Science and Myth." *Natural History,* 93:10-24, Nov. 1984.

Smith, John. *Generall Historie of Virginia, New England and the Summer Isles.* London: Michael Sparkes, 1624. Facsimile; Cleveland: World Publishing Co., 1966.

Soustelle, Jacques. *Daily Life of the Aztecs.* New York: Macmillan, 1965.

Speck, — —. "Bird Nomenclature of Canadian Delaware," *Journal of the Washington Academy of Sciences,* 36:8 p254.

Stiles, F. Gary. *Food Supply and the Annual Cycle of the Anna Hummingbird.* Berkeley: University of California Press, 1973.

Stoutenburgh, John. *Dictionary of the American Indian.* New York: Philosophical Library, Inc., 1960.

Stresemann, Erwin. *Ornithology from Aristotle to the Present.* Cambridge, MA: Harvard University Press, 1975. Original German text, Berlin, 1951.

Swan, James G. *Indians of Cape Flattery.* Seattle, Washington: Shorey Book Store, 1868. Facsimile, Smithsonian, 1964.

Thevet, André. *Les Singularités de la France Antarctique.* Paris: 1557. English translation by Thomas Hacket, London: H. Bynneman, 1568. University Microfilms, English Books 1475-1640, Reel 360: *The Newfounde Worlde or Anartike.*

Tyrell, Esther Q. and Robert A. *Hummingbirds.* New York: Crown Publishers, 1985.

United States Bureau of Ethnology. *Annual Reports* 1879-1916. Washington, DC: Government Printing Office, 1879-1916.

Vasquez, Fray Antonio de Espinosa. *Descriptions of the Indies.* Washington, DC: Smithsonian Institution Press (translation of original written in Spanish ca. 1600-22). First edition 1942; reprint 1968.

Verbeck, N. "Hummingbird feeding on sand." *Condor* 73, p112.

——— "Anna's Hummingbird Feeding." *Condor* 70, p273.

Verrill, A.H. *Isles of Spice and Palms.* New York: D. Appleton & Co., 1915.

Von Hagen, Victor. *Ancient Sun Kingdoms of the Americas.* Cleveland & New York: World Publishing Co., 1957-61.

Wagner, Henry R. "Peter Martyr and His Works." *American Antiquarian Society,* Oct. 1946, pp. 239-288.

Waser, Nikolas. "Pollen Shortcomings." *Natural History* 93:26-30, July 1984.

Waters, Frank. *Book of the Hopi.* New York: Viking, 1963.

Wilson, Alexander. *American Ornithology.* Philadelphia: Bradford & Inskeep, 1808-1813. Revision, Thomas Brewer, editor, Boston: Otis, Broaders & Co., 1840; facsimile, New York: Arno Press, 1970.

Wood, William. *New England's Prospects.* London: John Dawson, 1634. University Microfilms, English Books 1475-1640, Reel 980.

Wright, Barton. *Kachinas: A Hopi Artist's Documentary.* Flagstaff and Phoenix, AZ: Northland Press and Heard Museum, 1973.

Zimmerman, Dale. "Range Expansion of Anna's Hummingbirds," *American Birds,* 27:827-35, October 1973.

PERSONAL LETTERS

Baldwin, Bernice (Mrs. Robert): Makah Reservation, Neah Bay, Washington

Barros, Albert R.: Nez Perce Historical Park, Spalding, Idaho.

Bystrak, Danny: Bird Banding Laboratory, Laurel, Maryland.

Calder, William: Rocky Mountain Biological Laboratory, Crested Butte, Colorado, and University of Arizona.

Hutton, W.B.: formerly of a Chinook community in western Washington.

Lelooska: Amerind artist and historian, Ariel, Washington.

Schlick, Mary: Mount Hood, Oregon (Yakima affiliate).

Index